Legal Notice

This book is dedicated to all of our students, whose engagement inspires us every day. Remember, what your mind can conceive and believe your mind can achieve.

BOOKS FROM THE GET 800 COLLECTION FOR COLLEGE BOUND STUDENTS

28 New SAT Math Lessons to Improve Your Score in One Month
    Beginner Course
    Intermediate Course
    Advanced Course

New SAT Math Problems Arranged by Topic and Difficulty Level

New SAT Verbal Book for Reading and Writing Mastery

320 SAT Math Subject Test Problems Arranged by Topic and Difficulty Level
    Level 1 Test
    Level 2 Test

The 32 Most Effective SAT Math Strategies

SAT Prep Official Study Guide Math Companion

320 ACT Math Problems Arranged by Topic and Difficulty Level

320 AP Calculus AB Problems Arranged by Topic and Difficulty Level

320 AP Calculus BC Problems Arranged by Topic and Difficulty Level

555 Math IQ Questions for Middle School Students

555 Advanced Math Problems for Middle School Students

555 Geometry Problems for High School Students

Algebra Handbook for Gifted Middle School Students

Vocabulary Builder

CONNECT WITH DR. STEVE WARNER

www.facebook.com/SATPrepGet800
www.youtube.com/TheSATMathPrep
www.twitter.com/SATPrepGet800
www.linkedin.com/in/DrSteveWarner
www.pinterest.com/SATPrepGet800
plus.google.com/+SteveWarnerPhD

Vocabulary Builder

The Complete Vocabulary Word
Workshop for Building English
Vocabulary

Dr. Kazim Mirza   Dr. Steve Warner   Tana Cabanillas

Table of Contents

Actions to Complete Before You Read This Book   7

Actions to Complete After You Have Read This Book   188

ACTIONS TO COMPLETE BEFORE YOU READ THIS BOOK

1. Claim your FREE material

Visit the following webpage and enter your email address to receive Bonus Flashcards of the Hardest Words, plus more Vocabulary Games!

www.thesatmathprep.com/sat-vocab.html

2. 'Like' the Get 800 Facebook page

This page is updated regularly with test prep advice, tips, tricks, strategies, and practice problems. Visit the following webpage and click the 'like' button.

www.facebook.com/SATPrepGet800

INTRODUCTION

We have encountered words since the first day that we were born. Words can ignite a range of emotions from pure joy to anger and even indifference. We hope that this book incites a passion for words for the exam and beyond.

About the Book

This book is split into 3 sections. The first section breaks down the words into roots, prefixes and suffixes, as well as the hardest vocabulary words with activities for you to ingrain the words in your memory. The second section contains a workshop of practice of Verbal question types including fill in the blanks, short passage and long passage questions. The last section we encourage you to do after you mastered the first two sections. This section contains vocabulary games with the more challenging words.

This is not a book where we simply want you to memorize the definitions. We want to cultivate a love for the words and really have these words as part of your repertoire forever. These exercises will help you truly retain these words by creating many different connections in your brain. Learning words from different methods creates faster retrieval. And finally, we also advise to study continuously, as this is the most effective way to retain the information.

"Tell me and I forget. Teach me and I remember. Involve me and I learn." *Benjamin Franklin*

USING THIS BOOK EFFECTIVELY TO DOUBLE YOUR VOCABULARY IN ONE MONTH

The 100 most common Latin and Greek roots build more than 5,000 English words, which is just beyond half the average person's vocabulary of 10,000 words. The 100 most common Latin and Greek roots are the ones in all CAPITAL letters. By memorizing these 100 most common Latin and Greek prefixes, suffixes and roots, you will have the foundation in place to understand an additional 5,000 words. If you learn all of them (both the caps and non-caps roots), you can double this to 10,000 additional words!

Most of these roots are used in medicine, law, business, science and technology. And, you must know these roots in order to excel on English exams, conversational English, and working in an English speaking country. You must know the capital word's meanings. Many will not have the same exact meaning as the original Latin or Greek words but they will be close. The Romans also combined prefixes and roots to derive new words. Many were borrowed straight from the Greek language, but most were combined with Latin to make additional words with similar but distinctive meanings.

By breaking a word apart into root, prefix and suffix, you will be able to determine its literal meaning. Since you have encountered the word in context, you can then guess at its present meaning. For example, take the word "interposition." The prefix is 'INTER-', the suffix is '–ION' and the root word is 'POSIT'. Inter- means 'between', -ion is 'the act of' and 'POSIT' is from Latin meaning 'to place.' Therefore, 'interposition' literally means 'the act of placing between.' Another example is the word "antipathy." The prefix is 'ANTI-', the Greek root word is 'PATH' and the suffix is '-Y.' Anti- means 'against', the suffix,-y, is 'the state of' and PATH means 'to feel.' Antipathy therefore means 'the state of feeling against'. Not all derived words have both a prefix and a suffix, many will have one or the other, some will use just the root word and others will combine two root words, as in 'manuscript' and 'astronaut.' Man- is the Latin root for 'hand' and script is the Latin root 'to write.' Astro is the Greek word for 'star' and 'naut' means sailor.

The secret to increasing your vocabulary is not by memorizing a lot of words. The secret is in knowing how combining different prefixes and suffixes with a root word make new words. For example, let's take the Latin word gressum which means 'to walk, to step or move forward' and by combining the prefixes, A(D)-, CON-, DI-, E-, PRO-, RE-, RETRO- and TRANS- with the combining word "-GRESS-", we get 8 more words. If we add the suffixes –ION, -IVE, and –OR in turn to each of these words we derive 24 additional words for a total of 32 words. By knowing the meaning of the root word, and the 8 prefixes and 3 suffixes you also know the meaning of the 32 derived words. I use this example of making words to show you how easy it is to take words apart and thereby learn their meaning.

Since many Greek words were assimilated by the Romans and Latin words also come down to us through French, Italian and Spanish, the modern spelling of some of these words can be quite different from the original Latin or Greek. The Latin and Greek prefixes, suffixes and root words are listed alphabetically in Chapters 1-6.

After you've gone through the first six chapters, you can continue to practice doubling your vocabulary using your bonus vocabulary flashcards, found exclusively at

www.thesatmathprep.com/sat-vocab.html

Use your flashcards as a reference when going through Chapter 7, The Hardest Words. Most of the hardest words can be broken down into their Latin and Greek roots, then understood easily. Then, continue on to Part 2 and Part 3 of this book to apply what you've learned with vocabulary practice and games. Continue referring to your roots when you encounter an unfamiliar word. Chances are, you'll find that the word has a Latin or Greek root!

PART 1

2400 Vocabulary Words

"The habit of taking the path of least resistance makes all men, and some rivers, crooked."
Napoleon Hill

Chapter 1: Latin Prefixes

The prefixes listed below are from Latin prepositions. They are attached to nouns, adjectives and especially to verbs. When taking apart compound verbs and defining them, it is best to translate the prefix as adverbial rather than preposition. For example, abduct divides into ab (away) and duct (lead) and so means 'lead away' and not 'away from leading'. Some of these prefixes have different forms depending on the initial letter of the root word. This makes the derived word more pronounceable and is known as assimilation. A prime example is the prefix SUB- which also has SUC-,SUF-,SUG-,SUM-, SUP-, SUR-, and SUS- as different forms.

"Quod in vita faciamus, id in aeternitatem persistet."
"What we do in life, echoes in eternity." From the movie *Gladiator*

1. Latin Prefixes		
Prefix	Meaning	Examples
A-	not, without	amoral, APATHY, ANOMALY
AB-, ABS-	away from, off, apart	abrupt, ABSCOND, ABSTRACT
AD-, AC-, AN-, AS-	toward, against	advent, accurate, ANNOTATE, assent

AMBI-, AMB-	around, about, on both sides	AMBIGUOUS, AMBIVALENT
ANTE-	before, in front of, early	antecede, antedate, antebellum
ARCH	main, chief	archangel, archbishop, archenemy
BI-	two	bifurcate, biannually
BENE-	well	BENEFACTOR, benefit, beneficial
CIRCUM-, CIRA-	around, about	circumflex, circumference, circa
CIS-	on this side of	cisalpine
CON-	with, together	concur, concede, CONSCRIPT
COM-, COR-, COL-	together, with, very	COMPRISE, corrode, collateral
CONTRA-	against	contradict, controversy, contravene
COUNTER-	against	counterfeit, counterclockwise
DE-	down, down from, off, utterly	deformed, defoliate, descend, depress
DEMI-	half, partly belongs to	demisemiquaver, demigod

DIS-, DI-, DIF-	apart, in different directions	DIGRESS, divorce, dispute, DISCERN
DU-, DUO-	two	duet, duplicate
EM- EN-	in, into	embrace, enclose
EX-, E-, EF-, EC-	out, out of, from, away	EXTOL, event, expel, evade, ELUCIDATE
EXTRA-,EXTRO-	outside of, beyond	extraordinary, extrovert, EXTRAPOLATE
FORE	before	forestall, forgo, forebear
IN-, I-, IL-, IM-, IR-	in, into, on, toward, put into,	incision, impel, impulse, irrigate,
	not, lacking, without	illegal, ignominious, impure, immoral,
	same as above	immodest, indecent, INCOHERENT
INDU-, INDI-	a strengthened form of IN-	indigent
INFRA-	below, beneath, inferior to, after	infrared, infrasonic
INTER-, INTEL-	among, between, at intervals	intercede, intercept, intellect
INTRA-	in, within, inside of	intramural, intravenous
INTRO-	in, into, within	introduce, introspective

JUXTA	near, beside	juxtapose, juxtaposition
MAL-, MALE-	evil, badly	malformed, malicious, malaise, maladroit
MEDI-, MEDIO-	middle	median, mediocre
MONO-	one	MONARCH, MONOTONE
MULTI-, MULTUS-	much, many	multifaceted, multiply, multilevel
NE-	not	neuter, NEUTRAL
NON-	not (less emphatic than IN or UN)	nonresident, nonconformity
NUL-, NULL-	none, not any	nullify, nullification
OB-, OF-, OC-,	toward, against, across, down, for	oblong, OBDURATE, offer, occasion, occur
OP-, O-	toward, against, across, down, for	oppose, opposite, omit, offer
OMNI-	all, everywhere	omniscient, omnivorous
PED-, PEDI-	foot	pedestrian, pedicure
PER-, PEL-	through, by, thoroughly, away	PERMEATE, perfidy, pellucid
PRO-, PUR-	before, for, forth	proceed, purport, pursue, PROLONG
SE-, SED-	side, apart, away from	secure, seduce, seclude, sedition, select

SEMI-	half	semicircle, semiprivate
SINE	without	sinecure
SUB-, SUC-, SUF-	under, beneath, inferior,	suffer, SUBMISSIVE, succumb,
SUG-, SUM-, SUP-	less than, in place of, secretly	suggest, subtract, suffuse, support
SUR-, SUS-	(same as above meanings)	suspend, surplus
SUBTER-	beneath, secretly	subterfuge
SUPER-, SUPRA-	over, above, excessively	SUPERFICIAL, SUPERCILIOUS
SUR-	over, above, excessively	surcharge, surtax, surplus, surrealism
TRANS-, TRA-	across, over, beyond, through	transoceanic, transgression, transit, transition
ULTRA-	beyond, on other side	ultrasound, ultraconservative
UN- (Old English)	no, not, without	unabashed, unashamed

Chapter 2: Latin Suffixes

Latin Fun facts:

→ Latin study in high school has been shown to be linked statically to more successful college performance.

→ In Philadelphia, 20 minutes of Latin a day raised fifth grade reading scores in a full year.

→ English reading scores of Washington D.C. students were higher with one year of Latin than with four years of Spanish or French.

Latin Suffixes		
Suffix	**Meaning**	**Examples**
-ABLE, -ABLY	able to, capable of being.	unalienable, insuperable
-ACY	state or quality of being	intricacy, democracy
-AGE	belonging to, related to	marriage, acreage, postage
-AL	pertaining to, act of	infinitesimal, EPHEMERAL
-ANA	sayings, writings, facts of	Americana

-AN, -ANT, -ENT	one who is	charlatan, blatant, strident
-ANCE	act of, state of being, thing that	ABEYANCE
-ARY	Belonging to, a relation to.	hereditary, subsidiary
-ATE	having	alienate, incarnate, insensate
-ATION, -ITION	the act of, result of	alteration, compilation, nutrition
-AR	relating to, like; the nature of	singular, polar, vicar, scholar
-BULUM, -BLE	means, instrument, place	fable, stable
-CIDE, -CIDAL	killer; having power to kill	insecticide, suicidal
-CRAT, -CRACY	to govern	bureaucracy, plutocracy
-CULUM, -CLE	means, instrument, place	curriculum, fulcrum
-EN	to become, or cause to be	darken, weaken
-ENCE	act, fact, quality, state	conference, excellence, despondence
-ENCY	state of being	clemency, dependency
-ER, -OR	one who	interlocutor, volunteer

-ENT	has, shows, or does	circumvent, INADVERTENT
-ERY, -RY	a place to/for; occupation of	tannery, vinery, dentistry, jewelry
-ESCE	becoming	obsolescent, COALESCE
-FY	to make, cause to be, or become	CLARIFY, horrify
-HOOD	state, quality; group of	childhood, priesthood
-IAN	Belonging to, a relation to	egalitarian, plebian
-IER	a person concerned with	soldier
-IBLE	able to be.	susceptible, flexible
-IC	pertaining to	ASCETIC, PROSAIC, ENDEMIC
-ICE	state or quality of being	avarice
-IL, -ILE	having to do with	docile, missile, civil, fossil
-ION	the act or result of, one who	legion, opinion
-IUM, -Y, -CE, -GE	the act of	colloquium, colloquy, refuge
-CIUM, -TIUM, -	something	consortium, compendium

GIUM	connected with the act	
-ISH	of, or belonging to; like	devilish, boyish, foolish, bookish
-IST	a person who does, makes, practices	ALTRUIST, artist
-ITIOUS	having the nature of.	nutritious, seditious
-ITUDE, (-TUDE)	state of being.	verisimilitude, aptitude
-ITY	state, character, condition	ANIMOSITY, stability
-IVE	one who, that which is	pensive, ELUSIVE, deductive
-LESS	(OE) without, lacking.	relentless, tireless
-LIKE	characteristic of; suitable for	manlike, childlike, godlike
-LY	specified manner, extent, direction	harshly, hourly
-MEN	result, or means	acumen, specimen
-MENTUM, -MENT	result, or means of an act	armament, impediment, moment
-NESS	state, quality of being	Greatness. sadness

-OON	one who	buffoon
-OR	act, or condition of	error, terror, PRECURSOR
-ORY	relating to, thing which, place where	AMBULATORY, laboratory
-OSE, -OUS	having, full of, characterized by	IMPERVIOUS, unctuous, perilous
-SHIP	quality, condition, state of	fellowship, friendship
-SOME	like, tending to be	tiresome, lonesome
-TION	state of that which	convocation, commotion
-TUDE	state of being	verisimilitude, aptitude
-ULUS, -ULOUS	tending to	CREDULOUS, pendulous
-URE	state or act of	CENSURE, tenure
-UUS, -UOUS	tending to	INNOCUOUS
-VOROUS, -VORE	eating, feeding on	omnivorous, herbivore
-WISE	direction, manner, in regard to	clockwise
-Y	state of being.	nullity, APATHY

Chapter 3: Latin Base Words

Latin fun facts:

→ Our laws, government, art, architecture and even astronomy all have Roman origins.

→ Up to 80% of all words in languages such as Spanish, French, and Italian come from Latin.

Latin Base Words		
Latin word	Meaning	Examples
abstinere	to hold back	abstain, ABSTINENCE
accollare	to embrace	ACCOLADE
acerbus, AC, ACR	sharp, bitter, sour	acerbic, acrid, acumen, acrimony
actuare	to do, to move	ACTUATE
actus, ACT	drive, lead, to do, to act	active, activate, activism, react
acurer	to sharpen	ACUTE, acumen, acuity
adbaetere	witness, judge	ARBITER
adjacere	to lie near	adjacent
aemulus	trying to equal, excel	EMULATE
aequus	equal	EQUIVALENT

affecere, AFFE	a state of feeling, to feign	AFFECTATION, AFFECTED
ager, agri, agro, AGR	field	agronomy
agere, AG	drive, lead, to do, to act	agility, agitate, AGENDA
alacer	eager, quick, brisk	ALACRITY
albus	white	albino, albedo, albescent
alere, altum, AL, ALT	grow, nourish	alter
alius	other, else	alias, ALIENATE
alienus, ALIEN	of another, other	alien, alienation, unalienable
alludere	to joke, jest	allude, ALLUSION
alter, ALTER	other, another	alternative, altercation, ADULTERATE
alter	other of two	ALTERNATIVE
altus	high, deep	alto, altimeter, exaltation
amare, AM, AMAT	to love, friend	AMIABLE, enamored, amorous
ambulare, AMB	to walk, to go	amble, preamble, AMBULATORY
amicus	friend	AMITY
amplus	large, spacious	ample

anecdota	unpublished	ANCEDOTE
angere, anxius	to give pain	ANXIOUS, ANXIETY
angulus	a corner	angle, ANGULAR
anima	breath, spirit, soul	ANIMOSITY, inanimate, unanimous
animus, ANIM	reason, mind, soul, life	ANIMATE, magnanimous
annus, ANNU, ENNI	year	annual, biennial, centennial, PERENNIAL
anomalia	inequality	ANOMALY
antiquus	old, ancient	antiquity, antique, ANTIQUATED
apertum, APERT	open, uncovered	aperture
apparere	to come forth	apparent, appearance, APPARITION
appellare, APPELL	address, entreat, call	appellation
apprehendere	to take hold of	apprehend, APPREHENSIVE
apprenare	to teach	APPRISE
aptare, aptus, APT, EPT	to fit, suitable	aptitude, adapt, INEPT
arbit	judge	ARBITRATION, arbitrary
archein, ARCH	to rule	MONARCH

ardere ARD	be on fire, to burn	ardor, ARDUOUS
arere	to be dry	ARID
arguere	make clear	argument
arrogare	full of pride	ARROGANT, ARROGANCE
articulare	jointed; utter distinctly	ARTICULATE, inarticulate
artificium	art-craft + facere-to make	artifact, artifice, artificial
ascendere	to scale, climb	ascend, ASCENDANCY
aspergere	to sprinkle on	asperse, ASPERSION
assiduitas	constant presence	assiduity, ASSIDUOUS
astus	crafty, cunning	ASTUTE
auctor	author, enlarger	AUTHORITY, authorize
augere, AUG, AUX	to increase	AUGMENT, auxiliary
auctum, AUCT	increase	auction
auspicium	good omen, approval	auspice, AUSPICIOUS
authentious	real, genuine	AUTHENTIC
avarus	greedy	AVARICE, avaricious
avertere	to turn away	avert

26

bella, bellus	beautiful	EMBELLISH
bellum, BEL, BELL	to wage war	bellicose, rebellious, BELLIGERENT
bene, BEN	well, good	benevolence, BENEFICENT, BENIGN
bibere	to drink	bibulous, IMBIBE
blaterare	to babble, to roar	BLATANT
bonus, BON	good	bonanza, bonny, bon voyage, bonus
melior	better	AMELIORATE
brevis, BRI, BREV	brief, short	BREVITY, abbreviate, abridge
burla	a jest	BURLESQUE
cadere, CAD	to fall, happen by chance	DECADENT, cadaver, cascade
cidere, CID	to fall, happen by chance	coincidence, RECIDIVISM
casum, CAS	to fall, happen by chance	cascade
calere, CAL	be warm, glow	caloric, calorie
candere, CAND	glow, pure, sincere	incandescence, candor, CANDID
canere, CANT, CHANT	to sing	RECANT, chant, enchant

capere, CAP, CAPT	to take, to seize	captive, capture, intercept, CAPTIOUS
capra	a she goat (impulsive)	CAPRICIOUS, caprice
capere, CIP, CEPT	to take, to seize	INCIPIENT, precept, susceptible
caput, CAP, CAPIT	head, headlong	cape, chapter, capital, principle
castigare	to purify, chastise	CASTIGATE
causa	cause, reason	causal, causation
cavare, cavus	to make hollow	CAVERNOUS, cavity, excavate
cedere, CED, CEED	to go, to yield	recede, precede, exceed, PREDECESSOR
cessum, CESS	to go, to yield	concession, access, recess
censere, CENS	assess, rate, estimate	census, CENSURE
centrum, CENTR	center	concentric, concentrate, ECCENTRIC
cernere, CERN, CERT	distinguish, separate, decide	discern, certitude, DISCERNMENT
cerratanus	seller of Papal indulgences	CHARLATAN

cessare	to cease	INCESSANT
ciere, citum, CI	move, stir, rouse, call	cite, citation
citum, CIT	move, stir, rouse, call	excite, incite, SOLICIT, solicitous
civis	citizen, community	civic, civility, civilian
clamere, CLAIM	to shout, claim, cry out	CLARIFY, ACCLAIM, RECLAIM
clamatum, CLAM	to shout, claim, cry out	CLAMOR, PROCLAIM, declaration
clarus	bright, clear, famous	clarion, clarity
clausum, CLU	to close, shut	recluse, exclude, include, conclusion, PRECLUDE
clavis	key	clavicle, clavier, ENCLAVE
clemens	mild, merciful	CLEMENCY
clinatum, CLI, CLIN	lean, slope	incline, inclination, CLINOMETER
coagulare	to curdle	COAGULATE
codex, CODIC	book, tree trun	code, codicil
coercere	to surrond, restrain	COERCE
cogitare, COG	to think	COGENT, cogitative

cogitatum, COGITAT	to think	COGITATE
cognoscere, cognitum	to know	INCOGNITO, cognition, ignorant, COGNIZANT
colare	to strain, filter	percolate, colander
commodus	suitable	COMMODITY
complacere	to be pleased	complacency, COMPLAISANT
complere	to fill up	complete, comply, COMPLIANT
computare	to compute	count, DISCOUNT
comsentire (com + sentire)	to feel with	consent, CONSENSUS
concidere	to cut off	CONCISE
conciliare	bring together, win over	conciliate, CONCILIATORY, RECONCILE
conterere, contritio	ground to pieces, grief	CONTRITE, contrition
condensus	dense, compact	CONDENSE
condere	to put together, hide	RECONDITE
condescendere	to let oneself down	CONDESCEND

congruere	come together	CONGRUENT, INCONGRUOUS
contemnere	con-with + temnere-scorn	CONTEMPT
contendere	stretch out, strive after	CONTENTIOUS, contend, contention
copia	abundance	COPIOUS
cor, CORD, COUR	heart	courage, cordial, accord
corium	skin, hide	excoriate
cornu copia	(cornu) horn (copia) plenty	CORNUCOPIA
corona	crown	corona, coronary, coronation
corpus, CORPOR	body	corporeal, corporation
corroborare	to strengthen	CORROBORATE
corrumpere	destroy, spoil, bribe	CORRUPT
creare, CREA	create, grow	create, creative
crescere, CRESC	grow, increase	CRESCENDO, accretion
cretum, CRE, CRET	grow, increase	increase, increment
credere, CRED	to believe, to trust	credentials, incredible, credence

31

creditum, CREDIT	to believe, to trust	credit
cretum, CRET, CRIM	distinguish, separate, decide	secret, DISCRIMINATE, recrimination
crimen, CRIMIN	accusation, charge	incriminate, criminology
cruce	pot, jug	crucible
culminare	peak, summit	CULMINATE
culpa, CULP	fault, blame, guilt	culprit, CULPABLE, exculpate
cultus, CULT	to till, care	CULTIVATE, culture, cult
cumbere, CUB, CUMB	to lie down	incubate, recumbent, SUCCUMB
cura, CUR, CURAT	to care for	sinecure, secure
currere, CURR	to run	recur, current
cursum, CURS	to run	CURSORY, cursive
debilitare	to weaken	DEBILITATE
decorus	fit; proper	DECORUM, DECOROUS, indecorous
deffere	to bring down, yield	defer, DEFFERENCE
deliberare	to consider, weigh well	DELIBERATE

delirare	(to plow crooked) to rave	DELIRIUM, DELIRIOUS
deminuere	to lessen from	DEMINISH, diminutive
depravare	to make crooked	deprave, DEPRAVITY
determinare	to set bounds from	DETERMINED
devotus	to show reverence	devout, DEVOTION
dexter	right, right hand	dexterous, AMBIDEXTROUS
dicere, DIC	to say, to speak	indict, abdicate, PREDICAMENT
dictum, DICT	to say, to speak	dictate, verdict, edict, indict
dies,	day	diurnal
difficilis	hard to do	difficult
diffidere	to distrust	diffidence, DIFFIDENT
dignari	to consider, worthy	deign, DISDAIN, INDIGNANT
dignus, DIGN	worthy	dignify, dignitary, INDIGNANT
dilatare	dis-apart + latus-wide	dilate, dilation
distinguere	to separate	DISTINGUISHED
docere, DOC	teach	doctrine, document

doctum, DOCT	teach	doctor
dolere, DOL	be in pain, grieve	Doleful, dolorous. INDOLENT
dominus, dominium	a lord, right of ownership	domain, dominate, domineer
donare, DON, DOT	give, forgive	CONDONE, donation, donor
dotare	to endow	ENDOW, ENDOWMENT
dubius, DUB	doubt	DUBIOUS, indubitable
ducere, DUC	to lead	seduce, induce, SUBDUE
ductum, DUCT	to lead	conduct, ductile
durare, durus, DUR	to harden, hard	duress, OBDURATE, DURABLE, ENDURANCE
ebullire	to boil up	EBULLIENT
elicere	to draw out	ELICIT
emendare	to correct	EMEND, AMEND
enhaucere	to raise high	ENHANCE
equis, EQU, IQU	equal, even	equidistant, INIQUITY, equivalent
errare, ERR	wander, go astray	errant, error, err, ERRONEOUS
erudire	to instruct	ERUDITE
essentia	to be	ESSENCE, ESSENTIAL

ethicus	character, custom	ETHICAL
evitare	to shun, avoid	evitable, INEVITABLE
exhortari	ex-out + hortari- to urge	EXHORT, exhortation
exigere, exigens	to drive out	exigency, EXIGENT
exorbitare	to go out of the track	EXORBITANT
exponere	to put forth	expound, expose, EXPOSITION
expungere	mark for omission, erase	EXPUNGE
extirpare	to root out	EXTIRPATE
extraneare	to treat as a stranger	ESTRANGE
extremus	last, outermost	EXTREME, extremity
facilis	easy, to make easy	facile, facility, FACILITATE
facere, factum, FAC, FIC	to do, to make	facsimile, EFFACE, fiction, SURFEIT
facetia	a jest, witty	facetiae, FACETIOUS
fallere	to deceive, disappoint	FALLACIOUS, infallible

fari, FAB, FAM	speak	fame, fable, AFFABLE, famous
fastidium	loathing, disgust	FASTIDIOUS
fatuus	silly	FATUOUS, fatuity
fecundus	fertile, fruitful	FECUND, fatuity
femina	woman	female, feminine, femininity
fendere, FEND	to resist, hit, strike	defend, offend, offense
ferre, FER	to carry, to bear	refer, transfer, conference, proffer
fervere, FERV	boil, ferment	FERVOR, EFFERVESCENT, fervid
fetidus	to stink	FETID
fidere, fides, FID	faith, trust, rely on	fidelity, PERFIDY, perfidious, fiduciary
figare, fixus	to fasten, attach	fixative, crucifix, suffix
fingere	to touch, handle	feint, FEIGN
finis, FIN	end, limit	final, definite
flare, flatus	blow	deflate, inflation
flectere, FLECT	bend, turn	deflection, inflection, reflect
fligere, FLICT	to strike, drive, dash	afflict, inflict, conflict, PROFLIGATE
florere, FLOR-	thrive, to flower	FLOURISH, florid

fluitas, (superfluere)	to overflow	SUPERFLUOUS, SUPERFLUITY
foris	out of doors, beyond	FORFEIT, FORFEITURE
forma, FORM	shape, beauty, constant	UNIFORM, REFORM, FORMAL
fortis, FORT	strong, brave	fortify, force, forte, comfort, FORTITUDE
fortuna, FORT	chance, luck	fortunate, FORTUITOUS
fundare, FOUND, FUND	bottom	foundation, fundamental, PROFOUND
frangere, FRANG	to break	frangible, fragment
fraus, FRAUD	deceit, trickery	fraud, FRAUDULENT
frivolus	fragile, silly	FRIVOLOUS, frivolity
frugalis	proper, worthy	FRUGAL
fugere, FUG	flee, escape	fugacious
fugitum, FUGIT	flee, escape	fugitive
fulmen	lightning, thunderbolt	FULMINATE
fundere, FUND	to pour out, shed, scatter	refund, FUSILLADE
functum, FUNCT	perform, do, discharge	functionary
furere, FUR	rave, rage	fury, furious, infuriate

furtum	theft, stealthy	FURTIVE
fusum, FUS	pour, shed, scatter	diffuse, PROFUSE, effusive
futilis	worthless, untrustworthy	FUTILE, futility
garrire	chatter	GARRULOUS
genialis	of birth, generation	GENIAL, congenital, CONGENIAL
genus, GEN, GENER	birth, race, kind	GENRE, generic, generous, generation
gestum, GEST	carry, wear, wage	gestation, gesture
glutire	to devour	GLUTTON, gluttonous
gradior, GRAD, GRADI	walk, step; move foreward	gradual, retrograde, gradient
gressum, GRESS	walk, step; move foreward	progress, aggressive, REGRESS
gratus, GRAT	pleasing, favorable	gratitude, congratulate, INGRATIATE
gravis, GRAV, GRIEV	heavy, serious	grave, grievance, AGGRAVATE, gravid, grief, AGGRIEVE, GRAVITY
grex, GREG	flock, herd	congregate, segregate, GREGARIOUS

habere, HAB, habeo	to have, hold, keep	habit, inhabit
haerere, HER, HES	to cling, stick	adhesive, cohesive, adherent, INHERENT
haeresis	school of thought, sect	heretic, HERESY
harmonicus	fitting, agreement	HARMONY, harmonic
heres, HERED	heir	hereditary, heredity
herba	grass, herb	herbivorous, herbaceous
hilarare, hilaris	to gladden, merry	hilarious, exhilarate
histrio	actor	HISTRIONICS
homo, HOMIN	man, human being	homicidal, hominid
horrere, HORR	shudder, stand stiff	horrendous, abhor
hostis	enemy	hostile
humere, HUM	be moist, damp	humid
humilis	lowly	HUMILITY, humiliate
id	one's own	IDIOM, idiosyncrasy
ignis	fire	ignite, ignition, igneous
ignorare	to have no knowledge of	ignore, ignorant

imbuere	to wet, soak	IMBUE
immunis	tax exempt	IMMUNE
impedire (im + pes)	"to hold the feet", entangle	IMPEDE
imponere	to place upon	IMPOSE
inanis	empty, vacant	INANE
inchoare	to begin	INCHOATE
incurrere	to run into, attack	incur, INCURSION
indulgere	be kind to, yield to	Indulge. INDULGENT
iners (in + ars)	without skill or art	inertia, INERT
infere (in + ferre)	to carry in	INFER
ingenerare	to beset	ENGENDER
ingenuus	native, inborn, frank	INGENUOUS
inhibere	hold back, restrain	INHIBIT
inimicus	hostile	INIMICAL
iniquus	unequal	INIQUITY, INIQUITIOUS
inquirere	to seek	inquire, INQUISITIVE
insula, isola	island, to isolate	isolate, insulate, INSULAR
integritas	whole, entire	INTEGRITY

intendere	aim at, stretch for	intend, intense, INTENSIFY
intricare	to entangle, PERPLEX	INTRICATE, intricacy
intus	within	INTIMATE
iratus	to be angry	IRATE, IRASCIBLE
ire, itum, IT	to go	initiate, transit
iter, ITINER	journey, walk	ITINERANT
jacere, JAC	to throw, cast down	ejaculate, adjacent
jactum, JECT	to throw, cast down	eject, reject, trajectory, eject, object, OBJECTIVE
jejunus	hungry or meager	jejune
jocus	joke	jocund, jocular, jocose, jocosity
Jovis	Roman god Jupiter	JOVIAL
judex, JUDIC	judge, judgment	JUDICIOUS, judicial, adjudicate
jugum	a yoke	SUBJUGATE
jungere, JUNG	to join, to meet	conjugal, conjugate, CONJOIN
junctum, JUNCT	to join, to meet	junction, injunction

41

	right, law, take an oath	abjure, PERJURY, CONJURE, jurisprudence
jus, JUR, JUST		
juvenile	oung	juvenile, REJUVENATE
labi, LAB	slide, slip, fall	labile
labor	work, exertion	labor, laboratory, laborious
lacrima	a tear	lachrymal, lachrymose
lamentium	a mourning, wailing	LAMENT
languere	to be faint, listless	languid, LANGUISH, languor
lassus	faint, weary	LASSITUDE
latus, LATER	wide, sideways	LATITUDE. lateral, UNILATERAL
latere	to lie, hidden	LATENT
latum, -LAT	to bear, to carry	relate, translate
laudare	to praise, glory	LAUDABLE
lavere, LUT, LUG, LAV	to wash	dilute, DELUGE, lavatory
laxus	to be loose	LAX, laxity
legare	to send	RELEGATE, delegate
lethargia	idle	lethargic, LETHARGY
liber	free	liberate, libertine, deliberate
ligare	to bind	allegiance, oblige, ligature

ligne, LIGN	line, cord	align
lignum	wood	LIGNEOUS
linqua	tongue, language	linguistics, lingual
linquere, LINQU	leave, quit	relinquish
liquere, LIQU	to flow, be fluid, clear	liquid, PROLIX
litigare	to dispute	LITIGATE, LITIGANT
littera	letter of the alphabet	literature, obliterate, literal, literati
livere	be black and blue	livid
locus	place	dislocate, ALLOCATE
loquax, LOQUAC	talkative	LOQUACIOUS
loqui. LOQU	speak, talk	eloquent, soliloquy
locutum, LOCUT	speak, talk	elocution, CIRCUMLOCUTION
lucidus	light, clear	ELUCIDATE
ludere, LUD	to play, to mock	interlude, delude, ludicrous, elude, prelude
lugere, lugubris	to mourn	lugubrious
lusum, LUS	to play, to mock	illusion, COLLUSION
lumen	bright light	luminance, luminary, LUMEN

43

macer	lean, thin	MEAGER
macerare	make soft, or tender	MACERATE
magister, MAGISTR	teacher, master	magistrate
maximus, MAX	greatest, biggest, largest	maximum, maxim
manere, MAN	remain, dwell	manse, manor
mansum, MANS	remain, dwell	mansion
malleare	to beat with a hammer	MALLEABLE
malus, MAL	bad, evil, wrong	maladjusted, MALICE, malignant
malus, pejor	worse	PEJORATIVE
malus pessimus	worst	pessimist, pessimism, PESSIMISTIC
mandare (manus + dare)	to order, command	mandate, commandment, MANDATORY
manus, MAN, MANI	hand	manual, MANIFEST, manumit, manipulate
margo	borderland	margin, MARGINAL
mecari	to trade, buy	merchant, market
medius, mediocris	middle	intermediary, medieval, MEDIOCRE

melior	better	meliorate, AMELIORATE, melioration
mellifer	honey	MELLIFLUOUS
memoria, MEMIN	remember	memoir, memorable, memorandum
mendax, MENDAC	lying, false	mendacious, MENDACITY
mens	mind	mention
mensurare	to measure	measure, COMMENSURATE
merces	pay, wages	mercenary
mergere	to dip, sink	merge, MERGER
merx, MERC	goods, wares	merchant, merchandise
metus, meticulosus	fear, fearful	METICULOUS
migrare. MIGR	move, change places	emigrant
migratum, MIGRAT	move, change places	MIGRATORY, migration
minure	to lessen	DIMINISH
mirare	to look at, wonder at	mirage, miracle, admiral
miser	wretched, unhappy	MISER, miserable, miserly

miserari	to pity	misery, COMMISERATE
mitigare	to make mild, soft, tender	MITIGATE
mittere, MIT, MITT	send, let, go	emissary, remit, admittance, transmit
missum, MIS, MISS	send, let, go	missive, remission, demise, SURMISE
modestus	keeping due measure	MODEST, modesty
modus, MOD	measure, manner, means	mode, modal, modify
moles	mass, bulk, pile	molecule, molecular
monere, MON	to warn, advise, remind	monument, summons, remonstrate
monitum, MONIT	to warn, advise, remind	monitor, admonition, ADMONISH
mons, MONT	mountain	montage, monticule
morbus	disease	morbid
mordere, MORD	bite	REMORSE, mordacious
morsum, MORS	bite	morsel
morsus	peevish, fretful	MOROSE
mors, MORT	death, to die	immortal, morgue, MORBID, moribund
mos, MOR	manner, custom	MORALITY, mores

motum, MOT	to move	motion, motor, MOTIF
munificus	bountiful	MUNIFICENT
murmure	to murmur, roar	MURMUR
mus, MUR	mouse	murid, murine
musivus	artistic, of a muse	MOSAIC
nasci, NAT, NAS, NAI	to bear, be born	native, prenatal, natural, INNATE, RENAISSANCE
nativus	natural, native	NAÏVE, naiveté
negare	to deny	negation, abnegate
nemus, NEMOR	wood, grove	Nemophilist
nihil, NIHIL	none, nothing, not any	ANNIHILATE, nihilism, nil
nocere, NEC, NOC, NOX	to harm, injure	internecine, INNOCUOUS, obnoxious
norma	rule	normative
noster	ours	NOSTRUM
notum, NOT	know	notable, notation
novus, NOV, NOU	new, fresh	renovate, NOVICE, NOVEL
nox, NOCT	night	nocturnal, equinox
nullus, NUL, NULL	not any, none	null, annul, NULLIFY

47

numerou	number	enumerate, numerable, INNUMERABLE
numisma	a coin	numismatic, NUMISMATIST
nuntiare	to announce	DENOUNCE
nutrire	nourish	nutriment
nutiare, NOUNC, NUNC	to report, tell	announce, RENOUNCE, pronounce
nucella, nux, NUC	nut	nucleus, nuclear
obliterare	to blot out	OBLITERATE
obscurus	covered over	OBSCURE
obstare	to stand against, oppose	OBSTINATE
obviare	to prevent	OBVIATE
odium	hatred	odium, ODIOUS
officius	to do work	office, OFFICIOUS
ominosus	evil omen	OMINOUS
omnis, OMNI	all	omnipotent, omniscient
onus, ONER	burden	onerous, EXONERATE
optare	choose	option, opinion
opus, OPER	work	operative, opus, opera, operate
ordo, ORDIN	rank, row, order	ordinal
oriri, ORI	rise	origin, original

os, OSS	bone	osseous, OSSIFY
oscillare	to swing	OSCILLATE
ostendere	to show against	ostensible, OSTENTATION
palatum	to the palate	PALATABLE
pallere, PALL	be pale, yellow, or faded	PALLID, PALOR
par, parare	equal, to make equal	par, DISPARATE
paradigma	to show, example	PARADIGM
parcere	to spare	PARSIMONY
parens, parere	to appear	apparent, TRANSPARENT
parere, PAR	prepare, get ready, equal	DISPARATE, parity, preparedness
passus, pati, passum	suffer, endure	patient, PASSIVE, passion
pauci, PAU	few	PAUCITY, pauper
pauper, PO, POV, PU	poor person, poor	poverty, IMPOVERISH, pauper
pecunia	money	pecuniary, impecunious
pellere, PELL	driven, to push	compel, expel, propellant
pelsum, PULS	to push	pulsate, IMPULSIVE

49

pendere, PEND	to hang, weigh, play	impending, appendage, suspend, pending, PENCHANT
penser, pensum, PENS	to hang, weight, play	expense, dispense, pensive, indispensable
penuria	want, scarcity	PENURY, PENURIOUS
perfidia	faithlessness, to deceive	perfidy, perfidious
perfungi	get rid of, discharge	PERFUNCTORY
peroratus	to pray, speak, orate	PERORATE
perquisitum	something required	PERQUISETE
pervadere (per + vadere)	to go through	PERVADE, pervasive
pervius	per (through) via (way)	pervious, IMPERVIOUS
pessimus	worst	pessimist, pessimism, pessimistic
pestis	plague	pestilence, pestiferous, PESTILENT
petere, PET, PIT	aim at, seek, attack	impetuous, PETULANT, propitious

petitum. PETIT	aim at, seek, attack	petition
pius	devoted to duty, godly	PIOUS, piousness
placere, PLAC	please, be agreeable	PLACATE, placebo, IMPLACABLE
placitum, PLACIT	please, be agreeable	PLACID, COMPLACENT
plaudere, PLAUD	beat, clap, approve	applaud, plaudit, implode
plausum, PLAUS	beat, clap, approve, true	PLAUSIBLE
plexum, PLEX, PLIC	weave, plait, fold, tangle	complicate, IMPLICATE, complex
plenus,	full	plenty, replenish, PLETHORA
plicare, PLIC, PLICAT	to fold, bend	complicate, EXPLICIT, IMPLICIT
plere, PLE, PLET, PLEN	to fill, full	complete, IMPLEMENT, DEPLETE, replete
poenalis, PEN, PUN	to pay, compensate	penalty, punitive, penance
portio	share, portion	apportion, proportion
posterus	next, following	PREPOSTEROUS

potens	powerful, able	potentate, potent, potential
praedicare	to proclaim, declare	PREACH
precarius, PREC	to request, beg, prayer	precarious, imprecate
prediligere	to prefer	PREDILECTION
prehensum, PREHENS	seize, grasp	REPREHENSIBLE, COMPREHENSIVE, apprehend, comprehend
PRISE	seize, grasp	comprise, REPRISAL
pretiare, PREC	to value	precious, depreciation
privare	separate, peculiar	privilege, deprive
prodigere	wasteful	PRODIGAL
prodigiosus	marvelous	PRODIGIOUS, PRODIGY
profanus	before a temple	PROFANE, PROFANITY
promere	to bring forth	PROMPT
promittere	to promise	COMPROMISE
prope	near	approach, REPROACH
propendere	to hang or lean foreward	propend, PROPENSITY
propinquus	near	PROPINQUITY
prosa	direct speech	PROSE, PROSAIC

prosperare	succeed, thrive, grow	prosper, PROSPEROUS
providere, providens	to see before, cautious	provide, PRUDENT, providence, IMPROVIDENT
provincia	territory outside of Rome	province, PROVINCIAL
pudere, pudens	to feel shame, modest	IMPUDENT
pungere, PUNG	prick, sting	PUNGENT, EXPUNGE
pungere, POIGN, POINT	prick, sting	poignant, pointed
purgare	to clean	purge, purgatory
putris	rotten	putrid, PUTRIFY
quaesitum, QUIS	ask, seek	INQUISITIVE, exquisite, acquisition
qualis	of what sort, kind	QUALITY, QUALIFY
quies, QUI	quite	tranquil, ACQUIESCE, QUIESCENT
quotus	how many	QUORUM, quotient
radius	ray, beam, rod	radian, radiation
radix, RADIC	root	radicle, radical, ERADICATE
rancere, RANC	be stinking	rancid
raptum, RAPT	to seize, snatch	rapture, rapt
ratus	to reckon	RATIFY

raucus	to mutter, give hoarse cries	RAUCOUS
rectum, RECT	direct, in a straight line	rectitude
redundare	to overflow	REDUNDANT
refere, relatus	to bring back	refer, relate, CORRELATE
reformare	to make better	REFORM
refutare	to repel	REFUTE
regere, rectus	right, to make straight	erect, RECTITUDE
renda	to tear apart	rend
renuntiare	to tell back	RENOUNCE
repletus	to fill again	REPLETE, REPLETION
repellere	to repel, reject	repulse, repellent, repel
reprobare	rebuke, censure	REPROVE
repudiare	to put away, divorce	REPUDIATE
rescindere	to cut off	RESCIND
residere	remaining	residue, RESIDUAL
resilire	(salire) to jump, (re-) back	RESILIENT
respectus	to look at, look back on	respect, RESPITE

resplendere	shining brightly	RESPLENDENT
revelatio, revelare	disclose, reveal	REVELATION
rigere, RIG	to be stiff, numb	rigor, RIGOROUS, rigid, RIGIDTY
rogatum, ROGAT	ask, stretch out the hand	INTERROGATE, rogation, abrogate
rumpere, RUMP	to break, destroy	abrupt, rupture
ruptum, RUPT	to break, destroy	interrupt, CORRUPT, corruptive
sacrare, SANCT, SECR	holy	DESECRATE, CONSECRATE, sanctify
sacrare, SACR	holy	sacred, sacrament
sagax, sagacis, sapare	wise, to know, to taste	sage, SAGACIOUS, sapient
sanguis, SANGUIN	blood (cheerful)	SANGUINE, consanguinity
sapor, sapere	to taste	SAVOR, INSIPID
satis, satiare,	enough, to fill, full	sated, INIABLE, satisfy, satiate
satura	a satire, poetic medley	satire, IRIC
saquire	perceive clearly	SAGACIOUS
scala	stairs, ladder	SCALE

scandere, SCAND	climb	ascend, ascension, descendant
scire, SCI	to know, knowing	OMNISCIENT, science, conscious
scribere, SCRIB	write, incise, scratch	scribe, describe, TRANSCRIBE
scriptum, SCRIPT	write, incise, scratch	subscription, script, manuscript
scrupus	sharp stone	scruple, SCRUPULOUS
scrutari	to search into carefully	scrutiny, SCRUTINIZE
secare, SEC	to cut	section, sectional, sector
sectum, SECT	to cut	intersection
securus	free from care	secure, security
sedere, SED	to sit	sediment, preside, RESIDE
semen, SEMIN	to sow, seed	seminal, DISSEMINATE, SEMINARY
senex, SEN	old man	senate
sensus, SENSU	feeling	sensual
sentiere, SENT	to feel, perceive, think	SENTIENT, sentiment, consent, DISSENT
sequi, SEQ	to follow, following	SEQUENTIAL, sequence

secutum, SEC, SECUT	to follow	second, prosecute
serenus	dry, clear, calm	SERENE, SERENITY
servus	slave	SERVITUDE, service
sessum, SESS, SED, SID	to sit. plan, plot	session, preside, residual, subsidy
sidere	to settle	SUBSIDE
sinister	left-handed, unlucky	SINISTER
sinus	a bend	SINUOUS
sobrius	sober, moderate	SOBER, SOBRIETY
socius, sociare	companion, follower	society, social, association
solare, solus, SOL	to make lonely, alone	solo, SOLITARY, SULLEN
sollicitus	anxious, worried	SOLICIT, solicitous
soloecismus	speaking incorrectly	SOLECISM
solvere, SOLV	loosen, release, undo	solvent, resolve, INSOLVENT
somnus	sleep	somnolent, soporific
spirere, SPIR	to breathe, breath	aspire, INSPIRE
spiratum, SPIRAT	breath	respiration, inspiration

spondere, sponsus	to pledge, promise	sponsor, respond, RESPONSIVE
spurius	false, illegitimate	SPURIOUS
squalere, SQUAL	be rough, foul, or filthy	SQUALID, squalor
squandere	to scatter	SQUANDER
stare, stet, STA	to stand	stable, stagnant, contrast
stellare, stella	to shine, star	stellar, constellation
stinguere, STINGU	to prick, to quench	DISTINGUISH, EXTINGUISH
stinctum, -STINCT	to prick, to quench	distinct, distinction, distinctive
strategema	act of a general	strategy, STRATAGEM
stratum, STRAT	layer, spread	STRATIFY, STRATUM
striare	groove, channel, lined	STRIATED
stringere, STRING	draw tight, bind	astringent, STRINGENT
strictum, STRICT	draw tight, bind	strict, constriction
stridere	rasp	STRIDENT
suavis, SUA	sweet, smooth	suave, ASSUAGE, persuade
subtilis	fine, thin, precise	SUBTLE, subtlety
succedere	to go under, follow after	succeed, succession, SUCCESSIVE

succinctus	short, contracted	SUCCINCT
sumptus	expense, cost	SUMPTUOUS
superlatus	excessive	SUPERLATIVE
supplantare	to trip up	SUPPLANT
supponere	to suppose, assume	SUPPOSITION
surgere, surrection	to rise, risen	insurgency, INSURRECTION, resurrection
surrepticius	to take away secretly	SURREPTITIOUS
sycophania	informer, toady	SYCOPHANT
tacere, TAC, TIC	to be silent	TACIT, TACITURN, RETICENT
taedet	to disgust, offend	tedium, TEDIOUS
tangere, tactus, TANG	to touch	tangent, TANGIBLE, TANGENTIAL
temere, temeritas	rashly, blindly	TEMERITY
temetum	strong drink	ABSTEMIOUS
temnere	to scorn	contemn, CONTEMPT
temperare	to temper, mix, regulate	TEMPERATE, temperance, TEMPERAMENT
tempus. TEMPOR	time	temporal, contemporize, temporize

tendere, TEND	stretch, spread, aim	contend, tend, EXTEND, DISTEND
tentum, TENT, TEN	stretch, spread, aim	PRETENTIOUS, EXTENSIVE
tensum, TENS	stretch, spread, aim	tension, tensor
tendere	to stretch, extend, tend	tendency, TENDENTIOUS
tenere, TEN, TAIN	hold, keep	TENACIOUS, contain, detain, tenure
tentare, tent	to touch, try	TENTATIVE
tenuis, TEND, TENS	thin, stretched	extend, tenuous, tendency, tendon
tenuis, TENT, TENU	thin, stretched	tentative, contend, TENUOUS, extenuating
tepere	be lukewarm	tepid
terminus	boundary, end	terminator, terminal, DETERMINE
terere, TER, TRIT	rub away, tread, wear out	detriment
terrere, TERR	frighten	terror, DETER, terrorism
texere, textum, TEXT	weave, build	text, texture, textual, texturized
timere, TIM	fear	timid, TIMOROUS

tinctum, TINCT	dip, soak, moisten, dye	tincture
tirare	to draw fire	TIRADE
tirer	to draw	retire, RETIRING
trahere, TRA	to draw, drag	TRAIT, TRACE
tractum, TRACT	to draw, drag, pull	subtract, TRACTABLE, PROTRACT
transcendere	trans + scandere- to climb	transcend, transcendent
transigere	to come to a settlement	transact, INTRANSIGENT
trudere	to thrust	ABSTRUSE
truncus	stem, trunk	TRUNK, truncate, truncheon
trux, TRUC	wild, rough, fierce	TRUCULENT
trudere, TRUD, TRUS	to push, thrust	protrude, intrusion, UNOBTRUSIVE
tumere, TUM	swell, be swollen	tumescence, tumult, TUMOR
turba, TURB	uproar, disturbance	perturb, turbulence, turbid
turpis	base, vile	TURPITUDE
ultimus, ULTI	last	ultimate

umber (sub+umbrare)	shade, (under the shade)	SOMBER, ADUMBRATE
universus	all together	universal, universality, university
uniformis	one form, unchanging	UNIFORM, uniformity
uter	neither	neuter, NEUTRAL
vacare, vacuus	empty	VACUOUS, evacuate
vacillare	to stagger	VACILLATE
vadere, vasun, VAD	to go, make ones way	Vade mecum, EVADE, EVASIVE
vanescere	to vanish	EVANESCENT
varius	colored, DIVERSE	variable, variant, vary, VARIEGATED
vehemens	eager	VEHEMENT
vehere	carry	vehicle, vehicular
velle, volens	to wish, willing	VOLITION, BENEVOLENT
vena	blood vessel	vein, venous
vendere, VEND	sell	vend, vendor, venal
venenum	poison	venom, venomous
veneratus	to worship	VENERATE, veneration
venire, VENI, VEN	come, move toward	intervene, convention, CONTRAVENE

ventum, VENT, VENU	come, move toward	adventure, venue, invention
vereri	to feel awe	REVERE
vergere	to turn, bend	CONVERGE, DIVERGENT
vermis	worm	vermin, verminous
verus, VER	TRUE	VERIFY, aver, verdict, VERACITY
versum, VERS	to turn, change	versatile, AVERSION, DIVERSE
vertere, VERT, VER	to turn, change	revert, introvert, subvert, introversion, diverse, DIVERT
verticalis	the top, turning point	VERTICAL, VERTEX
vexare, VEX	shake, toss, trouble	VEX
visum, VIS, VIEW	to see	visual, visible, review, supervise, VISIONARY
vigere, VIG	thrive, flourish	vigorous, VIGOR
vincere, VINC	conquer, win	invincible, convince, CONVICTION
vindicta	revenge, to claim, avenge	VINDICTIVE, VINDICATE

vir, virtus	man, manliness, worth	virtue, VIRTUOUS, triumvirate
voluntas	free will	VOLUNTARY, VOLUNTEER
volvere, volutum	to turn	revolve, devolve, revolt, voluble
vorere	to eat, devour	VORACIOUS, carnivore, omnivorous
vocalis, vox, VOC	voice	vocal, vocalize
volo, VOL	to wish, to will	VOLUNTARY, VOLITION
votum, VOT	promise, wish, vow	vote, votive, vow

Chapter 4: Greek Prefixes

"I'll tell you a secret. Something they don't teach you in your temple. The Gods envy us. They envy us because we're mortal, because any moment might be our last. Everything is more beautiful because we're doomed. You will never be lovelier than you are now. We will never be here again." From the movie *Troy*

Greek prefixes		
Word	Meaning	Examples
DEUTERO-	second, farther	Deuteronomy
DIA-, DI-	through, across	diagram, dialysis, DIALECT, dialogue
DIS-, DI-	two, through, across	dilemma, dissect
DYS-	bad, difficult, faulty	dysfunctional (ill-, un-, mis-)
EC-, EX-	out, from, off	exit
ECO-	environment, habitat	ecosphere, ecosystem, ecotype
ECTO-	on the outside, without	ectoderm, ectomorph
EN-, EM-	in, into	energy
ENDO-	within, inside, internal	endocrine, endocardium
ENNEA-	nine	ennead

65

EPI-, EP-	upon, at, over, near	epicenter, EPISODE, epidermis
ESO-	inward, within	esoteric, esophagus
EU-	good, well	EUPHONY, euphemism, eugenics, euphoria
EXO-	outside, external	exoteric, exclude
HECATO-	hundred	hecatomb
HEMI-	half	hemisphere
HEPTA-	seven	heptagon
HETERO-	unlike, other	heterogeneous, HETERODOXY
HEXA-	six	hexagon
HIER-	sacred	HIEROGLYPHICS
HOLO-	whole	holistic
HOMEO-	like, similar	HOMEOPATHY, HOMEOSTASIS
HOMO-	like, similar	homogeneous, homonym
HYPER-	over, above, beyond	hyperactive, HYPERBOLE
HYPO-	under, less than	HYPOCRITE, hypodermic, HYPOTHETICAL
IDIO-	individual	IDIOSYNCRASY
IDEO-	idea	ideologue

ISO-	equal	isometric, isobar
KILO-	thousand	kilogram, Kilohertz
MACRO-	large	macroscopic
MEGA-, MEGALO-	large	megaton, megalopolis, MEGALOMANIA
MESO-	middle	Mesolithic, mesoderm
META-	among, between, beyond	metathesis, metaphysical
MICRO-	small	microscopic
MONO-	one	monorail
MYRIAD-	ten thousand	MYRIAD
NEO-	new	neoclassical
PENTA-	five	pentagon, pentagram
PERI-	around, about	perimeter, PERIPHERY, perihelion, perigee
PROS-	to, toward, besides	prostrate
SYN-, SYM-, SYS-	together, with	symmetric, SYNOPSIS, SYNTHESIS
TELE-	far, distant	telephone, telegraph
TELEO-	end, result	teleology
TRI-	three	trimester

Chapter 5: Greek Suffixes

Greek fun facts:

→ The Ancient Greeks were the first Europeans to read and write with an alphabet

→ The word ALPHABET derives from the first two letters of the Greek Alphabet (alfa - beta)

Greek suffixes		
Suffix	Meaning	Examples
-AC, -IAC	pertaining to	cardiac, hypochondriac
-AST	one who does	scholiast
-CRACY	government	democracy
-EMIA	condition of the blood	anemia
-GENESIS	creation, formation	parthenogenesis
-GENIC	suitable	photogenic
-GRAM	record	electrocardiogram
-GRAPH	written	monograph, telegraph
-GRAPHY	process/method of writing	photography, calligraphy
-IA, -Y	act, state of	polity, EUPHORIA, dyslexia

-IATRICS	treatment of disease	pediatrics
-IATRY	healing	psychiatry
-IC	pertaining to, one who	DOGMATIC, aristocratic
-ICAL	pertaining to, made of	political, angelical
-IC, -ICE	art, science, study of	politics
-INE	used to form feminine nouns	heroine
-ITE	inhabitant of, product	sybarite, Lucite
-ITIS	inflammation	tendonitis, bronchitis, neuritis
-ISE, -IZE	to make to give	PROSELYTIZE, sanitize
-ISK, ISCUS	little	asterisk
-ISM	the belief in, profession of	hylozoism, euphemism, baptism
-IST	one who believes in	Platonist
-LATRY	worship of	idolatry
-LYSIS	loosening	analysis
-MA, -M, -ME	result of	dogma, theorem, theme

-MANCY	prophecy	necromancy
-MANIA	madness for	pyromania
-METER	to measure	centimeter
-OID	resembling, like, shaped	humanoid, android
-OLOGY	science or study of	geology
-OMA	tumor	melanoma
-OSIS	abnormal condition	halitosis
-SCOPE	instrument for visual exam	telescope, microscope
-SIS	act, state of	metamorphosis
-TIC	pertaining to	STATIC, enigmatic
-Y	state of being	ANTIPATHY

Chapter 6: Greek Base Words

Greek fun facts:

→ About 12% of the English vocabulary, mainly technical and scientific terms, derives from Greek. e.g mathematics, astronomy, geography, biology, politics, democracy, athletics, marathon, technology, electricity, antibiotics, telephone

→ Almost every English word that starts with PH is of Greek origin. e.g philosophy, physical, photo, phrase, phoneme, phobia, phenomenon, philanthropy

Greek base words		
Word	Meaning	Examples
aesth, AESTH	feeling	AESTHETICS
aer, AER	lower air	aerobic, aerodynamic
agogos, AGOG	leader	DEMAGOGUE, pedagogic
agon, AGON	contest, struggle	antagonist, agony
agro, agros	field, earth, soil	agriculture, agronomy
algia	pain	neuralgia
allos, ALLO	other	allotropic, allomorph, allopathic, allogamy
athl	prize	decathlon

ainigma	riddle	ENIGMA, enigmatic
archos, ARCH	chief, first, rule	monarch, archangel, archipelago, ANARCHY
aristo, aristos	best	aristocracy, aristocrat
auto, autos, AUTO	self	autoimmune, autobiography
axioma	authority, to think worthy	AXIOM
ballein, BAL	throw	ball, ballistics
bat, BAT	go	acrobat
batho, BATHO	depth	bathysphere
biblos, BIBLIO, BIBL	book	bibliography, bible
blasphemein	to slander	BLASPHEMY
caco	bad, poor, evil	CACOPHONY
CAUT, CAUST	burn	cauterize, CAUSTIC
center	center	center
cephal	head	encephalitis
CLIN	lean	incline, thermocline
CRAT, CRAS	type of government	bureaucrat, theocracy, democracy
CRIT	judge	criticize

crypto, CRYPT	hide, conceal	ENCRYPTION, CRYPTOGRAM
Cynicus	a Greek philosopher	CYNIC, cynicism
demos, DEM, DEMO	the people	ENDEMIC, demographic, democrat
diatribe	a wearing away	DIATRIBE
didakikos	apt at speaking	DIDACTICS
doxo, DOX	belief, opinion	ORTHODOX, HETERODOXY, doxology
dran, DRA	to do, act	DRAMATIZE
EP,	word	epigraph
ephemeros	for the day, short lived	EPHEMERAL, ephemeris, ephemeron
episteme	knowledge	EPISTEMOLOGY
esoteikos	belonging to inner circle	ESOTERIC
esthesia	feel sensation	anesthesia, AESTHETICS
ETHER	upper air	ETHEREAL
ethnos, ETHN	nation, people	ethnic
ETYM	root	etymology
exo	outside	Exorcist
geno, GEN	kind, type, race	gender, Genesis

ge, GEO	earth	geography, geodesic, geometry, apogee,
glossal, GLOT	language	polyglot, glossary, epiglottis
GLYPH	carving	HIEROGLYPHICS, petroglyph
GNO, GNOS,	know	diagnosis, ignore, incognito, cognitive
gonos	to produce	cosmogony, astrogony
hedonikos	pleasure	hedonic, HEDONISTIC, hedonism
helios, HELIO	sun	heliocentric, heliotrope, aphelion
helix, HELIC	spiral	helix, helicoid
hemisus, hemi-	half	hemisphere
hiero	sacred, holy	HIEROGLYPHIC
histanai, STA, STE	stand	STATIC
hybris	exaggerated pride	HUBRIS
hypocrita	stage actor	HYPOCRITE, HYPOCRISY
isos, ISO	equal, alike	isometric, isotope
k(c)ine, KINE, CINE	movement	kinesthetic, cinema
k(c)lastes	breaker, broken	ICONOCLAST

K(C)LINO, CLI	to bend, slant	inclination, declination, decline, recline
k(c) risis, CRIT	to sift, separate	crisis, criterion, critic, critical
lakon	a Lanconian, Spartan	LACONIC
legein	to choose, pick	LOGIC
lemma	proposition	DILEMMA
lithos, LITH	stone	megalith
logos, -LOG	word, reason, study	monologue, logic
malagma	an emollient	AMALGAM
misein, MIS, MISO	hate	MISANTHROPE, misogynist
necro	death, corpse	necropolis, necrosis
nom	rule	ANOMALY, ANOMALOUS
nomos	law, science	astronomer
nostos	a return	NOSTALGIA
oikos	house	ecology
opsis, optic	sight, view, eye	optician, optical, SYNOPSIS, SYNOPTIC
orthos	right, correct	orthogenesis
pas, PAN, PANT	all, entire, every	panoply, PANDEMONIUM, pantheon

PATH	disease	PATHOLOGY, PATHOGEN
pathos, PATHO	feeling, suffering	EMPATHY, ANTIPATHY, SYMPATHY
ped, PED	child, instruction	pediatric, encyclopedia, PEDAGOGUE
periphos	moving around	periphery, PERIPHERAL
petros, PETR	rock, stone	petrified
phago, PHAG	eat, eating	phagocyte, esophagus
PHAN	show, make appear	phantom, fantasy, emphasis
philos, PHIL	love, tendency	philharmonic, philately, philosophy, bibliophile
phobos, PHOB	fear, flight	zoophobia
phone, PHON	voice, sound	phonograph, telephone, EUPHONY,CACOPHONY
plethore	to be full	PLETHORA
PLUT	wealth	plutocrat
pneuma, PNEUM	wind, spirit	pneumatic
polemikos, polemos	a war	POLEMIC
polit, polis	city	cosmopolitan, metropolitan
prattein, PRAG	do	PRAGMATIC, pragmatism
poblema	to throw forward	problem, PROBLEMATIC

pro	first	prototype, proton, protozoa
pseudes, PSEUDO	FALSE	pseudoscience, pseudointellectual
RHEA, RHAG	flow, gush, break	diarrhea, hemorrhage
schisma, SCHIS, SCHIZ	cleave, split	schism, schist, schizophrenic
scopos	to watch, see	telescope
SKEP, SCOP	examine, look at	SKEPTICAL, scope
sophos, SOPH	wise	sophisticated, sophomoric, sophist
stizein, STIG	mark, tattoo	STIGMA
stoa	porch, a covered walk with columns	Stoicism, STOIC, stoical
STROPH	turn	catastrophe
TACT, TAX	arrangement	tactics, syntax
TELE	far away	telemetry, telescope
temno, tomos, temnein, TOM	cut, cut off	appendectomy, lobotomy
thanatos	death	Euthanize, thanatology, EUTHANASIA
theos, THEO	god	THEOLOGY, atheist, theocracy
thesis	position	SYNTHESIS, thesis

tonos, TON	tone	monotone, TONIC
topo, TOP	place	topography, topic
TROPH	nourish	ATROPHY
typos	type, model	typify, typical, atypical
xenos, xeno	stranger	xenophobia, xenophobia, xenia
zelos	ardor, zeal	ZEALOUS, zealot

Chapter 7: The Hardest Vocab Words

These are the hardest words found in English language. Study the word, pronunciation, part of speech, and how the words are used in a sentence. Be sure to complete the activities for each word to help you remember them!

supercilious

sōopər͟'silēəs

adjective

behaving or looking as though one thinks one is superior to others.

"a supercilious lady's maid"

My friend is incapable of hiding her _____ smile when she sees the beggar on the street, as if thinking to herself that she is so much better off than him.

latin = supercilium = eyebrow

negative charge

antonym: humble modest

synonym: haughty patronizing imperious

* If you were to make an association w/ the word CILIA (latin: eyelash but in Biology: hairlike organelles) and the word supercilious it would be _____. *Hint: Cilia in the lungs "brush off" germs.*

dictum

diktəm

noun

a formal pronouncement from an authoritative source, important idea or rule

"the First Amendment dictum that "Congress shall make no law … abridging the freedom of speech""

latin = dic = something said

There are many unspoken _____ that we have to adhere to if we don't want to get fired.

synonym: proverb, maxim

antonyms:

positive charge

*Give an example of a dictum that you would like to break without consequences.

aloof

ə'lōof

adjective

not friendly or forthcoming; cool and distant.

"they were courteous but faintly aloof"

The term was originally an adverb in nautical use, meaning 'away and to windward'

negative charge

synonym: distant cold

antonyms: warm friendly

Recount an experience where a person was aloof towards you.

prudent

prōodnt

adjective

acting with or showing care and thought for the future.

"no prudent money manager would authorize a loan without first knowing its purpose"

latin = prudentia = foreseeing, attending to, knowledge

synonym: cautious, carefulness

antonym: recklessness, brash

positive charge

* In most movies, we have a variety of characters (selfish, loving, immature...), can you think of a character that was prudent?

loquacious

lō'kwāSHəs

adjective

tending to talk a great deal; talkative.

latin = loqui = to talk

negative charge

The stock character in every sitcom is the adorable yet loquacious neighbor who loves to barge in.

What is a Loquacious Sesquipedalian?

decorus

di'kôrəs

adjective

in keeping with good taste and propriety; polite and restrained, honor

"dancing with decorous space between partners"

synonyms: proper, seemly, decent, becoming, befitting, tasteful antonyms: unseemly

latin = decorous = appropriate

How does this word relate to soldiers?

capricious

kəˈpriSHəs

adjective

given to sudden and unaccountable changes of mood or behavior.

"a capricious and often brutal administration"

synonyms: fickle, inconstant, changeable, variable, mercurial,

volatile, unpredictable, temperamental; whimsical, fanciful

"the capricious workings of fate"

antonyms: consistent

What is the Arbitrary and Capricious Law?

stratagem

stratəjəm

noun

a plan or scheme, especially one used to outwit an opponent or

achieve an end.

"a series of devious stratagems"

synonyms: plan, scheme, tactic, maneuver, ploy, device, trick,

ruse, plot, machination, dodge; subterfuge, artifice, wile;

"Warren devised a series of stratagems to win their confidence"

Origin

late 15th century (originally denoting a military ploy): from French

stratagème, via Latin from Greek stratēgēma, from stratēgein 'be

a general,' from stratēgos, from stratos 'army' + agein 'to lead.'

What was Russia's genius stratagem that ultimately defeated Napoleon Bonaparte?

jingoism

jiNGgō͵izəm

noun

extreme patriotism, especially in the form of aggressive or warlike foreign policy.

synonyms: extreme patriotism, chauvinism, extreme nationalism, xenophobia, flag-waving; hawkishness, militarism, belligerence, bellicosity

"a newspaper known for its jingoism"

How is Jesus and the word Jingo related?

bureaucratization

byŏŏrə'kratik

adjective

relating to the business of running an organization, or government.

"well-established bureaucratic procedures"

overly concerned with procedure at the expense of efficiency or common sense.

"the plan is overly bureaucratic and complex"

Out of the three models of bureaucracy which do you like best?

milieu

mil'yŏŏ

noun

a person's social environment.

"he grew up in a military milieu"

synonyms: environment, sphere, background, backdrop,

setting, context, atmosphere; location, conditions, surroundings, environs; informal: stomping grounds, stamping grounds, turf

"the political milieu in New England"

What is milieu therapy?

---

edifying

edə͵fī

instruct or improve (someone) morally or intellectually.

synonyms: educate, instruct, teach, school, tutor, train, guide; enlighten, inform, cultivate, develop, improve, better

"students who have no desire to be edified should leave my classroom and take up thumb-twiddling"

What is an moral experience in which you learned through trial & error and not per instruction?

---

retrench

ri'trenCH

verb

reduce or diminish (something) in extent or quantity.

"right-wing parties which seek to retrench the welfare state"

synonyms: reduce, cut, cut back, cut down, pare, pare down, slim down, make reductions in, make cutbacks in, trim, prune; shorten, abridge

"services have to be retrenched"

How does this word relate to employment?

---

preeminence

prē'emənəns

noun

the fact of surpassing all others; superiority.

"the region has never regained the economic preeminence that it once enjoyed"

synonyms: superiority, supremacy, greatness, excellence, distinction, prominence, predominance, eminence, importance, prestige, stature, fame, renown, celebrity

"the preeminence of Flemish and Dutch painters was unchallenged"

What is The Preeminence of Reason (The importance of reason)?

effusive

iˈfyo͞osiv

adjective

expressing feelings of gratitude, pleasure, or approval in an unrestrained or heartfelt manner: "an effusive welcome".

synonyms: gushing, gushy, unrestrained, extravagant, fulsome, demonstrative, lavish, enthusiastic, lyrical.

antonyms: restrained.

Can you relate the word fuse and effusive?

incorrigible

inˈkôrijəbəl

adjective

not able to be corrected, improved, or reformed.: "she's an incorrigible flirt".

synonyms: inveterate, habitual, confirmed, hardened, dyed-in-the-wool, incurable, chronic, irredeemable, hopeless, beyond hope.

antonyms: repentant.

A teen can be deemed incorrigible by law, what are the different type of sentences that the teen face?

tenuous

tenyōoəs

adjective

very weak or slight.: "the tenuous link between interest rates and investment".

synonyms: slight, insubstantial, meager, flimsy, weak, doubtful, dubious, questionable, suspect.

antonyms: convincing, strong.

Can you distinguish between the words tenuous and tentative?

ineffable

in'efəbəl

adjective

too great or extreme to be expressed or described in words.: "the ineffable natural beauty of the Everglades".

synonyms: indescribable, inexpressible, beyond words, beyond description, begging description.

Recount a memory which was beyond words.

sullen

'sələn

adjective

bad-tempered and sulky; gloomy.: "a sullen pout".

synonyms: surly, sulky, pouting, sour, morose, resentful, glum, moody, gloomy, grumpy, bad-tempered, ill-tempered.

antonyms: cheerful.

Give shade (of meaning) to the following: sullen, glum, morose, sulky.

dissent

di'sent

verb

hold or express opinions that are at variance with those previously, commonly, or officially expressed.: "two members dissented from the majority" "there were only a couple of dissenting voices".

In your opinion, is dissent truly the highest form of patriotism?

divisive

di'vīsiv

adjective

tending to cause disagreement or hostility between people.: "the highly divisive issue of abortion".

synonyms: alienating, estranging, isolating, schismatic.

antonyms: unifying.

What are the top 3 divisive topics that is hard to bring up with your best friend?

bucolic

byoo'kälik

adjective

of or relating to the pleasant aspects of the countryside and country life.: "the church is lovely for its bucolic setting".

synonyms: rustic, rural, pastoral, country, countryside.

Does bucolic and colic come from the same word?

lugubrious

lə'g(y)oobrēəs

adjective

looking or sounding sad and dismal.

synonyms: mournful, gloomy, sad, unhappy, doleful, glum, melancholy, woeful, miserable, woebegone, forlorn, somber, solemn, serious, sorrowful, morose, dour, cheerless, joyless, dismal.

antonyms: cheerful.

Did Salvador Dali really emote gloominess when he made "lugubrious game"

remonstrance

ri ˈmänstrəns

noun

a forcefully reproachful protest.: "angry remonstrance in the Senate" "he shut his ears to any remonstrance"

How are demonstrance and remonstrance similar?

erudition

er(y)o͝o͵diSHən

noun

the quality of having or showing great knowledge or learning; scholarship.: "he was known for his wit, erudition, and teaching skills".

synonyms: knowledge, scholarship, learning, intelligence, intellect.

antonyms: ignorance.

Is the following quote from Abigail Adams "You have overburdened your argument with ostentatious erudition?" a jab towards her husband?

lassitude

lasə͵t(y)o͞od

noun

a state of physical or mental weariness; lack of energy.: "she was overcome by lassitude and retired to bed" "a patient complaining of lassitude and inability to concentrate".

synonyms: lethargy, listlessness, weariness, languor, sluggishness, tiredness, fatigue, torpor, lifelessness, apathy.

antonyms: vigor

How is Lassitude related to Multiple Sclerosis?

miscreants

miskrēənt

Latin : mis dis creante believing : not believing

noun

a person who behaves badly or in a way that breaks the law..

synonyms: criminal, culprit, wrongdoer, malefactor, offender, villain, lawbreaker, evildoer, delinquent, hoodlum, reprobate.

Who were the miscreants in the movie Tangled?

equitable

ekwitəbəl

adjective

fair and impartial.: "an equitable balance of power".

synonyms: fair, just, impartial, even-handed, unbiased, unprejudiced, egalitarian.

antonyms: unfair.

When you win a lawsuit there are two different types of claims equitable and legal claims. What are the differences?

concord

käNG‚kôrd

noun

agreement or harmony between people or groups.: "a pact of peace and concord".

synonyms: agreement, harmony, accord, consensus, concurrence, unity.

antonyms: discord

Cord means heart which is part of the word concord, what part of the heart still has the word "chordae (heart)" in it.

inane

i'nān

adjective

silly; stupid.: "don't constantly badger people with inane questions".

synonyms: silly, foolish, stupid, fatuous, idiotic, ridiculous, ludicrous, absurd, senseless, asinine, frivolous, vapid.

antonyms: sensible.

What does Volucella inanis mean? And how does it relate to the word inane?

byzantine

bizən͵tēn

adjective

(of a system or situation) excessively complicated, typically involving a great deal of administrative detail.: "Byzantine insurance regulations".

synonyms: daedal, complicated, convoluted, difficult

antonyms: Apparent, clear, simple, uncomplicated

What was the Byzantine Empire, and when did they rule?

onerous

ōnərəs

adjective

(of a task, duty, or responsibility) involving an amount of effort and difficulty that is oppressively burdensome.: "he found his duties increasingly onerous".

synonyms: burdensome, arduous, strenuous, difficult, hard, severe, heavy, back-breaking, oppressive, weighty, uphill, challenging, formidable, laborious, Herculean, exhausting, tiring, taxing, demanding, punishing, grueling, exacting, wearing, wearisome, fatiguing.

antonyms: effortless, easy.

Have you ever had a class that felt onerous from the beginning? What class was it?

Arcane

ärˈkān

adjective

understood by few; mysterious or secret.: "modern math and its arcane notation".

synonyms: mysterious, secret.

Do you have any arcane jokes with your friends? Thinking of it will help you remember this word.

abstruse

abˈstrōos

adjective

difficult to understand; obscure.: "an abstruse philosophical inquiry".

synonyms: obscure, arcane, esoteric, little known, recherché, rarefied, recondite, difficult, hard, puzzling, perplexing, cryptic, enigmatic, Delphic, complex, complicated, involved, over/above one's head, incomprehensible, unfathomable, impenetrable, mysterious.

didactic

dīˈdaktik

adjective

intended to teach, particularly in having moral instruction as an ulterior motive.: "a didactic novel that set out to expose social injustice".

synonyms: instructive, instructional, educational, educative, informative, informational, edifying, improving, pedagogic, moralistic.

consecrate

känsiˌkrāt

Verb

make or declare (something, typically a church) sacred; dedicate formally to a religious or divine purpose.: "the present Holy Trinity church was consecrated in 1845" "consecrated ground".

seditious

siˈdiSHəs

Adjective

inciting or causing people to rebel against the authority of a state or monarch.: "the letter was declared seditious".

synonyms: rabble-rousing, provocative, inflammatory, subversive, troublemaking.

corollar

kôrəˌlerē

Noun

a proposition that follows from (and is often appended to) one already proved.

"job losses are the unfortunate corollary of budget cutting"

---

enigma

iˈnigmə

Noun

a person or thing that is mysterious, puzzling, or difficult to understand.

synonyms: mystery, puzzle, riddle, conundrum, paradox, problem, quandary.

Greek ainigma, from ainissesthai 'speak allusively'

What is an enigma machine? How did it relate to WWII?

---

apparition

apəˈriSHən

Noun

a ghost or ghostlike image of a person.

synonyms: ghost, phantom, specter, spirit, wraith.

Apparition is considered a way of magical traveling in the Harry Potter Series. How does this relate to the traditional word.

---

disingenuous

disinˈjenyo͞oəs

Adjective

not candid or sincere, typically by pretending that one knows less about something than one really does.

synonyms: insincere, dishonest, untruthful, false, deceitful, duplicitous, lying, mendacious

Recall a time when you received a disingenuous apology.

precipitate

adjective

done, made, or acting suddenly or without careful consideration.: "I must apologize for my staff—their actions were precipitate".

synonyms: hasty, overhasty, rash, hurried, rushed.

How does precipitate relate to rain?

contentious

Adjective

kənˈtenCHəs

causing or likely to cause an argument; controversial.: "a contentious issue".

synonyms: controversial, disputable, debatable, disputed, open to debate, vexed.

Please explain the idiom "bone of contention".

subversive

Adjective

səbˈvərsiv

seeking or intended to disrupt an established system or institution.: "subversive literature"

synonyms: disruptive, troublemaking, inflammatory, insurrectionary.

Relate the words sedition, treason and subversive actions, which one in your opinion is worse?

lament

Verb

ləˈment

mourn (a person's loss or death).: "he was lamenting the death of his infant daughter".

synonyms: mourn, grieve, sorrow, wail, weep, cry, sob, keen, beat one's breast.

antonyms: celebrate, rejoice.

Laments are considered one of the oldest types of poem in human history, where these poems sung by men or women?

cataclysmic

Adjective

katəˈklizmik

relating to or denoting a violent natural event.

Have you ever been present in a cataclysmic event? Recount your experience.

inimitable

in·im·i·ta·ble

Adjective

iˈnimitəbəl

so good or unusual as to be impossible to copy; unique.: "the inimitable ambience of Hawaii".

synonyms: incomparable, unparalleled, unrivaled, peerless, matchless, unequaled, unsurpassable, superlative, supreme, perfect, beyond compare, second to none, in a class of one's own.

What are The Society of Inimitable Livers?

incongruous

in·con·gru·ous

Adjective

inˈkäNGgro͞oəs

not in harmony or keeping with the surroundings or other aspects of something.: "the duffel coat looked incongruous with the black dress she wore underneath".

synonyms: out of place, out of keeping, inappropriate, unsuitable, unsuited.

antonyms: appropriate.

How can triangles be compared as incongruent.

---

scrupulous

scru·pu·lous

Adjective

skro͞opyələs

(of a person or process) diligent, thorough, and extremely attentive to details.: "the research has been carried out with scrupulous attention to detail".

synonyms: careful, meticulous, painstaking, thorough, assiduous, sedulous, attentive, conscientious, punctilious, searching, close, minute, rigorous, particular, strict.

antonyms: careless.

---

magnanimous

mag·nan·i·mous

Adjective

magˈnanəməs

very generous or forgiving, especially toward a rival or someone less powerful than oneself.

synonyms: generous, charitable, benevolent, beneficent, big-hearted, handsome, princely, altruistic, philanthropic, unselfish, chivalrous, noble.

antonyms: mean-spirited, selfish.

Has anyone ever done something that you saw as so incredibly generous that you felt the person was magnanimous?

impugns

im·pugn

Verb

im'pyo͞on

dispute the truth, validity, or honesty of (a statement or motive); call into question.: "the father does not impugn her capacity as a good mother".

synonyms: call into question, challenge, question, dispute, query, take issue with.

cosmopolitan

cos·mo·pol·i·tan

Adjective

käzmə'pälitn

familiar with and at ease in many different countries and cultures.: "his knowledge of French, Italian, and Spanish made him genuinely cosmopolitan".

synonyms: worldly, worldly-wise, well-travelled, experienced, cultivated, cultured, sophisticated, suave, urbane, glamorous, fashionable, stylish.

carp

Verb

kärp

complain or find fault continually, typically about trivial matters.: "I don't want to carp about the way you did it" "he was constantly carping at me".

synonyms: complain, cavil, grumble, grouse, whine, bleat, nag.

antonyms: praise.

pragmatic

prag·mat·ic

Adjective

prag'matik

dealing with things sensibly and realistically in a way that is based on practical rather than theoretical considerations.: "a pragmatic approach to politics".

synonyms: practical, matter-of-fact, sensible, down-to-earth, commonsensical, businesslike, having both/one's feet on the ground, hardheaded, no-nonsense.

antonyms: impractical.

synesthesia

syn·es·the·sia

Noun

sinəs'THēZHə

the production of a sense impression relating to one sense or part of the body by stimulation of another sense or part of the body.

subordinate

sub·or·di·nate

Adjective

sə'bôrdnit

lower in rank or position.: "his subordinate officers".

synonyms: lower-ranking, junior, lower, supporting.

antonyms: senior.

recant

re·cant

Verb

ri'kant

say that one no longer holds an opinion or belief, especially one considered heretical.: "heretics were burned if they would not recant" "Galileo was forced to recant his assertion that the earth orbited the sun".

synonyms: renounce, disavow, deny, repudiate, renege on.

truncate

trun·cate

Verb

trəNG͵kāt

shorten (something) by cutting off the top or the end.: "a truncated cone shape" "discussion was truncated by the arrival of tea".

synonyms: shorten, cut, cut short, curtail, bring to an untimely end.

antonyms: lengthen, extend.

vacuity

va·cu·i·ty

Noun

va'kyo͞oətē

lack of thought or intelligence; empty-headedness.: "full of excitement, I listened to my first student sermon – only to be taken aback by its vacuity".

empty space; emptiness.

drudgery

drudg·er·y

Noun

drəjərē

hard, menial, or dull work.: "domestic drudgery".

synonyms: hard work, menial work, donkey work, toil, labor.

prescient

pre·scient

Adjective

preSH(ē)ənt

having or showing knowledge of events before they take place.: "a prescient warning".

synonyms: prophetic, predictive, visionary.

ornate

or·nate

Adjective

ôrˈnāt

made in an intricate shape or decorated with complex patterns.: "an ornate wrought-iron railing".

synonyms: elaborate, decorated, embellished, adorned, ornamented, fancy, fussy, ostentatious, showy.

antonyms: unadorned.

multifarious

mul·ti·far·i·ous

Adjective

məlt(ə)ˈfe(ə)rēəs

many and of various types.: "multifarious activities".

anachronism

a·nach·ro·nism

Noun

əˈnakrəˌnizəm

a thing belonging or appropriate to a period other than that in which it exists, especially a thing that is conspicuously old-fashioned.: "everything was as it would have appeared in centuries past apart from one anachronism, a bright yellow construction crane".

byzantine

Byz·an·tine

Adjective

bizənˌtēn

(of a system or situation) excessively complicated, typically involving a great deal of administrative detail.: "Byzantine insurance regulations".

adroit

a·droit

Adjective

əˈdroit

clever or skillful in using the hands or mind.: "he was adroit at tax avoidance".

synonyms: skillful, adept, dexterous, deft, nimble, able, capable, skilled, expert, masterly, masterful, master, practiced, handy, polished, slick, proficient, accomplished, gifted, talented.

antonyms: inept, clumsy.

---

nefarious

ne·far·i·ous

Adjective

niˈfe(ə)rēəs

(typically of an action or activity) wicked or criminal.: "the nefarious activities of the organized-crime syndicates".

synonyms: wicked, evil, sinful, iniquitous, egregious, heinous, atrocious, vile, foul, abominable, odious, depraved, monstrous, fiendish, diabolical, unspeakable, despicable.

antonyms: good.

---

slipshod

slip·shod

Adjective

slipˌSHäd

(typically of a person or method of work) characterized by a lack of care, thought, or organization.: "he'd caused many problems with his slipshod management".

synonyms: careless, lackadaisical, slapdash, disorganized, haphazard, hit-or-miss, untidy, messy, unsystematic, unmethodical, casual, negligent, neglectful, remiss, lax, slack.

antonyms: meticulous.

---

artifice

ar·ti·fice

Noun

rtəfis

clever or cunning devices or expedients, especially as used to trick or deceive others.: "artifice and outright fakery" "the style is not free from the artifices of the period".
synonyms: trickery, deceit, deception, duplicity, guile, cunning, artfulness, wiliness, craftiness, slyness, chicanery.

circumlocutions
cir·cum·lo·cu·tion
Noun
sərkəm͵lōˈkyo͞oSHən
the use of many words where fewer would do, especially in a deliberate attempt to be vague or evasive.: "his admission came after years of circumlocution" "he used a number of poetic circumlocutions".
synonyms: periphrasis, discursiveness, long-windedness, verbosity, verbiage, wordiness, prolixity, redundancy, pleonasm, tautology, repetitiveness, repetitiousness.

reproach
re·proach
Verb
riˈprōCH
address (someone) in such a way as to express disapproval or disappointment.: "critics of the administration reproached the president for his failure to tackle the deficiency" ""You know that isn't true," he reproached her".

whimsical
whim·si·cal
Adjective

wimzikəl

playfully quaint or fanciful, especially in an appealing and amusing way.: "a whimsical sense of humor".

synonyms: fanciful, playful, mischievous, waggish, quaint, quizzical, curious, droll, fantastical, Seussian.

discrete

dis·crete

Adjective

dis'krēt

individually separate and distinct.: "speech sounds are produced as a continuous sound signal rather than discrete units".

synonyms: separate, distinct, individual, detached, unattached, disconnected, discontinuous, disjunctive, disjoined.

antonyms: connected.

crude

Adjective

kro͞od

constructed in a rudimentary or makeshift way.: "a relatively crude nuclear weapon".

synonyms: primitive, simple, basic, homespun, rudimentary, rough, rough and ready, rough-hewn, make-do, makeshift, improvised, unfinished, jury-rigged, jerry-built, slapdash.

antonyms: sophisticated.

(of language, behavior, or a person) offensively coarse or rude, especially in relation to sexual matters.: "a crude joke".

synonyms: vulgar, rude, naughty, suggestive, bawdy, off-color, indecent, obscene, offensive, lewd, salacious, licentious, ribald,

coarse, uncouth, indelicate, tasteless, crass, smutty, dirty, filthy, scatological.
antonyms: decent, inoffensive.

abstractions
ab·strac·tion
Noun
abˈstrakSHən
the quality of dealing with ideas rather than events.: "topics will vary in degrees of abstraction".

narrative
nar·ra·tive
Noun
narətiv
a spoken or written account of connected events; a story.: "the hero of his modest narrative".
synonyms: account, chronicle, history, description, record, report, story.

cryptic
cryp·tic
Adjective
kriptik
having a meaning that is mysterious or obscure.: "he found his boss's utterances too cryptic".
synonyms: enigmatic, mysterious, confusing, mystifying, perplexing, puzzling, obscure, abstruse, arcane, oracular, Delphic, ambiguous, elliptical, oblique.
antonyms: clear.

solemn

sol·emn

Adjective

säləm

formal and dignified.: "a solemn procession".

synonyms: dignified, ceremonious, ceremonial, stately, formal, courtly, majestic.

antonyms: frivolous.

condescending

con·de·scend·ing

Adjective

kändəˈsendiNG

having or showing a feeling of patronizing superiority.: "she thought the teachers were arrogant and condescending" "a condescending smile".

synonyms: patronizing, supercilious, superior, snobbish, snobby, disdainful, lofty, haughty.

aesthetic

aes·thet·ic

Adjective

esˈTHetik

concerned with beauty or the appreciation of beauty.: "the pictures give great aesthetic pleasure".

evoke

e·voke

Verb

iˈvōk

bring or recall to the conscious mind.: "the sight of American asters evokes pleasant memories of childhood".

synonyms: bring to mind, put one in mind of, conjure up, summon (up), invoke, elicit, induce, kindle, stimulate, stir up, awaken, arouse, call forth.

sophistry

soph·ist·ry

Noun

säfəstrē

the use of fallacious arguments, especially with the intention of deceiving.

disparage

dis·par·age

Verb

diˈsparij

regard or represent as being of little worth.: "he never missed an opportunity to disparage his competitors".

synonyms: belittle, denigrate, deprecate, trivialize, make light of, undervalue, underrate, play down.

antonyms: praise, overrate.

curtail

cur·tail

Verb

kərˈtāl

reduce in extent or quantity; impose a restriction on.: "civil liberties were further curtailed".

synonyms: reduce, cut, cut down, decrease, lessen, pare down, trim, retrench.

antonyms: increase.

epitome

e·pit·o·me

Noun

iˈpitəmē

a person or thing that is a perfect example of a particular quality or type.: "she looked the epitome of elegance and good taste".

synonyms: personification, embodiment, incarnation, paragon.

proponents

pro·po·nent

Noun

prəˈpōnənt

a person who advocates a theory, proposal, or project.: "a collection of essays by both critics and proponents of graphology".

synonyms: advocate, champion, supporter, backer, promoter, protagonist, campaigner, booster, cheerleader.

debunk

de·bunk

Verb

diˈbəNGk

expose the falseness or hollowness of (a myth, idea, or belief).: "the magazine that debunks claims of the paranormal".

synonyms: explode, deflate, quash, discredit, disprove, contradict, controvert, invalidate, negate.

antonyms: confirm.

acumen

a·cu·men

Noun

əˈkyo͞omən

the ability to make good judgments and quick decisions, typically in a particular domain.: "business acumen".

synonyms: astuteness, shrewdness, acuity, sharpness, sharp-wittedness, cleverness, smartness, brains.

partisanship

par·ti·san·ship

Noun

pärtəzənˌSHip

prejudice in favor of a particular cause; bias.: "an act of blatant political partisanship".

synonyms: bias, prejudice, one-sidedness, discrimination, favor, favoritism, partiality, sectarianism, factionalism.

intemperance

in·tem·per·ance

Noun

inˈtemp(ə)rəns

lack of moderation or restraint.: "his occasional intemperance of tone".

irreverence

ir·rev·er·ence

Noun

iˈrev(ə)rəns

a lack of respect for people or things that are generally taken seriously.: "an attitude of irreverence toward politicians".

lucid

lu·cid

Adjective

lo͞osid

expressed clearly; easy to understand.: "a lucid account" "write in a clear and lucid style".

synonyms: intelligible, comprehensible, understandable, cogent, coherent, articulate.

antonyms: confusing, ambiguous.

bright or luminous.: "birds dipped their wings in the lucid flow of air".

esoteric

es·o·ter·ic

Adjective

esə'terik

intended for or likely to be understood by only a small number of people with a specialized knowledge or interest.: "esoteric philosophical debates".

synonyms: abstruse, obscure, arcane, recherché, rarefied, recondite, abstract.

openhanded

o·pen·hand·ed

Adjective

ōpən'handid

giving freely; generous.: "openhanded philanthropy".

synonyms: generous, magnanimous, charitable, benevolent,

beneficent, munificent, bountiful, liberal, unstinting.

antonyms: tightfisted, stingy.

---

constituent

con·stit·u·ent

Adjective

kənˈstiCHo͞oənt

being a part of a whole.: "the constituent minerals of the rock".

synonyms: component, integral.

being a voting member of a community or organization and having the power to appoint or elect.: "the constituent body has a right of veto".

---

magnanimity

mag·na·nim·i·ty

Noun

ˌmagnəˈnimətē

the fact or condition of being magnanimous; generosity.: "both sides will have to show magnanimity".

---

solicitous

so·lic·i·tous

Adjective

səˈlisitəs

characterized by or showing interest or concern.: "she was always solicitous about the welfare of her students" "a solicitous inquiry".

synonyms: concerned, caring, considerate, attentive, mindful, thoughtful, interested.

---

fissure

Verb

fiSHər

split or crack (something) to form a long narrow opening.: "the skin becomes dry, fissured, and cracked".

trivializes

triv·i·al·ize

Verb

trivēəˌlīz

make (something) seem less important, significant, or complex than it really is.: "the problem was either trivialized or ignored by teachers".

synonyms: treat as unimportant, minimize, play down, underestimate, make light of, treat lightly, dismiss, underplay, downplay, diminish, belittle.

morbid

mor·bid

Adjective

môrbəd

characterized by or appealing to an abnormal and unhealthy interest in disturbing and unpleasant subjects, especially death and disease.: "he had long held a morbid fascination with the horrors of contemporary warfare".

synonyms: ghoulish, macabre, unhealthy, gruesome, unwholesome.

antonyms: wholesome.

gloating

Verb

glōt

contemplate or dwell on one's own success or another's misfortune with smugness or malignant pleasure.: "his enemies gloated over his death".

synonyms: delight, relish, take great pleasure, revel, rejoice, glory, exult, triumph, crow.

menial

me·ni·al

Adjective

mēnēəl

not requiring much skill and lacking prestige.: "menial factory jobs".

synonyms: unskilled, lowly, humble, low-status, inferior, degrading.

erratic

er·rat·ic

Adjective

iˈratik

not even or regular in pattern or movement; unpredictable.: "her breathing was erratic".

synonyms: unpredictable, inconsistent, changeable, variable, inconstant, irregular, fitful, unstable, turbulent, unsettled, changing, varying, fluctuating, mutable.

antonyms: consistent.

tactful

tact·ful

Adjective

tak(t)fəl

adroitness and sensitivity in dealing with others or with difficult issues.: "they need a tactful word of advice" "they were too tactful to say anything".

synonyms: diplomatic, discreet, considerate, sensitive, understanding, thoughtful, delicate, judicious, politic, perceptive, subtle.

resolute

res·o·lute

Adjective

rezə͵lo͞ot

admirably purposeful, determined, and unwavering.: "she was resolute and unswerving".

synonyms: determined, purposeful, resolved, adamant, single-minded, firm, unswerving, unwavering, steadfast, staunch, stalwart, unfaltering, unhesitating, persistent, indefatigable, tenacious, strong-willed, unshakable.

antonyms: halfhearted.

autonomy

au·ton·o·my

Noun

ôˈtänəmē

(of a country or region) the right or condition of self-government, especially in a particular sphere.: "Tatarstan demanded greater autonomy within the Russian Federation".

efface

ef·face

Verb

i'fās

erase (a mark) from a surface.: "with time, the words are effaced by the frost and the rain" "his anger was effaced when he stepped into the open air".

synonyms: erase, eradicate, expunge, blot out, rub out, wipe out, remove, eliminate.

make oneself appear insignificant or inconspicuous.

synonyms: make oneself inconspicuous, keep out of sight, keep out of the limelight, lie low, keep a low profile, withdraw (oneself).

crush

Noun

krəSH

a crowd of people pressed closely together, especially in an enclosed space.: "a number of youngsters fainted in the crush".

synonyms: crowd, throng, horde, swarm, sea, mass, pack, press, mob.

Verb

krəSH

deform, pulverize, or force inwards by compressing forcefully.: "you can crush a pill between two spoons" "the crushed remains of a Ford Bronco".

synonyms: squash, squeeze, press, compress.

abstracted

ab·stract·ed

Adjective

ab'straktid

showing a lack of concentration on what is happening around

one.: "she seemed abstracted and unaware of her surroundings" "an abstracted smile".

synonyms: absent minded, distracted, preoccupied, in a world of one's own, with one's head in the clouds, daydreaming, dreamy, inattentive, thoughtful, pensive, lost in thought, deep in thought, immersed in thought, in a brown study, musing, brooding, absent, oblivious, moony, distrait.

antonyms: attentive.

musing

mus·ing

Noun

myo͞oziNG

a period of reflection or thought.: "his musings were interrupted by the sound of the telephone".

synonyms: meditation, thinking, contemplation, deliberation, pondering, reflection, rumination, introspection, daydreaming, reverie, dreaming, preoccupation, brooding.

sanctity

sanc·ti·ty

Noun

saNG(k)titē

the state or quality of being holy, sacred, or saintly.: "the site of the tomb was a place of sanctity for the ancient Egyptians".

synonyms: holiness, godliness, blessedness, saintliness, spirituality, piety, piousness, devoutness, righteousness, goodness, virtue, purity.

contented

con·tent·ed

Adjective

kənˈtentəd

happy and at ease.: "I felt warm and contented".

adept

a·dept

Adjective

əˈdept

very skilled or proficient at something.: "he is adept at cutting through red tape" "an adept negotiator".

synonyms: expert, proficient, accomplished, skillful, talented, masterly, masterful, consummate, virtuoso.

antonyms: inept.

congenial

con·gen·ial

Adjective

kənˈjēnyəl

(of a person) pleasant because of a personality, qualities, or interests that are similar to one's own.: "his need for some congenial company".

synonyms: hospitable, genial, personable, agreeable, friendly, pleasant, likable, amiable, nice.

antonyms: disagreeable.

reclusive

re·clu·sive

Adjective

ri'kloōsiv

avoiding the company of other people; solitary.: "a reclusive life in rural Ireland".

synonyms: solitary, secluded, isolated, hermitlike, hermitic, eremitic, eremitical, cloistered.

antonyms: gregarious.

---

pilfer

pil·fer

Verb

pilfər

steal (typically things of relatively little value).

synonyms: steal, thieve, take, snatch, purloin, loot.

---

predilection

pre·di·lec·tion

Noun

predl'ekSHən

a preference or special liking for something; a bias in favor of something.: "my predilection for Asian food".

synonyms: liking, fondness, preference, partiality, taste, penchant, weakness, soft spot, fancy, inclination, leaning, bias, propensity, bent, proclivity, predisposition, appetite.

antonyms: dislike.

from Latin praedilect- 'preferred,' (prae 'in advance' + diligere 'to select.')

---

penchant

pen·chant

Noun

a strong or habitual liking for something or tendency to do something.: "he has a penchant for adopting stray dogs".

synonyms: liking, fondness, preference, taste, relish, appetite, partiality, soft spot, love, passion, desire, fancy, whim, weakness, inclination, bent, bias, proclivity, predilection, predisposition.

profundity

pro·fun·di·ty

noun

deep insight; great depth of knowledge or thought.: "the simplicity and profundity of the message".

anachronism

a·nach·ro·nism

Noun

a thing belonging or appropriate to a period other than that in which it exists, especially a thing that is conspicuously old-fashioned.: "everything was as it would have appeared in centuries past apart from one anachronism, a bright yellow construction crane".

Greek anakhronismos, from ana- 'backward' + khronos 'time.'

perquisites

per·qui·site

noun

another term for perk.

a thing regarded as a special right or privilege enjoyed as a result of one's position.

"the wife of a president has all the perquisites of stardom"

afflictions

af·flic·tion

Noun

something that causes pain or suffering.: "a crippling affliction of the nervous system".

synonyms: disorder, disease, malady, complaint, ailment, illness, indisposition, handicap.

allusion

al·lu·sion

noun

an expression designed to call something to mind without mentioning it explicitly; an indirect or passing reference.

synonyms: reference to, mention of, suggestion of, hint to, intimation of, comment on, remark on

"the town's name is an allusion to its founding family"

heretic

her·e·tic

Noun

a person holding an opinion at odds with what is generally accepted.

synonyms: dissenter, nonconformist, apostate, freethinker, iconoclast; agnostic, atheist, nonbeliever, unbeliever, idolater, idolatress, pagan, heathen.

antonyms: conformist, believer

invocation

in·vo·ca·tion

Noun

the action of invoking something or someone for assistance or as an authority.: "the invocation of new disciplines and methodologies".

estrangement

es·trange·ment

noun

the fact of no longer being on friendly terms or part of a social group.: "the growing estrangement of the police from their communities".

synonyms: alienation, antagonism, antipathy, disaffection, hostility, unfriendliness.

stresses (multi-definition)

intense effort

pressure

synonym: emphasize

antonym: deemphasize

The stresses from the weather really strained the foundation of the house.

aspersions

aspercio : a sprinkling

a sprinkling of water in religious ceremony

an intentional false statement meant to harm's one reputation

The aspersions were quite effective, he plans to leave the company as soon as he can.

Can you find how both definition relates to each other? Clue the latter definition started in the mid-17th century.

Bonus: which idiom is correct? To cast dispersion or cast aspersions?

elucidate

lucidus: lucid

To make clear

synonym: illuminate

antonym: obscure

There is nothing like a color atlas to help elucidate what the text could not.

nihilism

The belief that traditional values/belief has no basis and useless

nihil: nothing

Scott has a tendency to be nihilistic when he doesn't win a game, his attitude unfortunately spreads to his work too.

What is existential nihilism?

cacophony

kako: bad

phony: sound

discordant sounds

Synonyms : clamor

Antonym : euphony

The cacophony of sounds coming from the room has lead me to believe that the violin was only meant to torture human souls.

Can you find a cacophonous and euphonious song?

paucity

pacus: little

smallness of quality

syn: lack

antonym: abundance

Paucity doesn't even begin to describe the lack of affection given to this emaciated child.

libelous

li·bel

lībəl

noun

liber= book

a published false statement that is damaging to a person's reputation; a written defamation.

synonyms: defamation, defamation of character, character assassination, calumny, misrepresentation, scandalmongering.

"a counselor who sued two national newspapers for libel"

Activity: What is the difference between libel and slander?

disparaging

dis·par·ag·ing

Verb

di'sparij

to extract

lower in rank

regard or represent as being of little worth: "he never missed an opportunity to disparage his competitors".

The disparaging comments did not dissuade the fighter, he fought with unparalleled might.

synonyms: belittle, denigrate, deprecate, trivialize, make light of, undervalue, underrate, play down.

antonyms: praise, overrate.

Latin = par = equal

Can actors use the non-disparagement clause?

conflagration

con·fla·gra·tion

Noun

känflə'grāSHən

an extensive fire that destroys a great deal of land or property.

synonyms: fire, blaze, flames, inferno, firestorm.

"the conflagration spread rapidly through the wooden buildings"

Latin = con = with + Latin = flagrare = to blaze

truculent

truc·u·lent

Adjective

trəkyələnt

eager or quick to argue or fight; aggressively defiant.: "his days of truculent defiance were over".

synonyms: defiant, aggressive, antagonistic, combative, belligerent, pugnacious, confrontational, ready for a fight, obstreperous, argumentative, quarrelsome, uncooperative.

antonyms: cooperative, amiable.

Latin truculentus, from trux, truc- 'fierce.'

What was the HMS Truculent? How does it relate to its definition?

affable

af·fa·ble

Adjective

afəbəl

friendly, good-natured, or easy to talk to.: "an affable and agreeable companion".

synonyms: friendly, amiable, genial, congenial, cordial, warm, pleasant, nice, likable, personable, charming, agreeable, sympathetic, simpatico, good-humored, good-natured, jolly, kindly, kind, courteous, civil, gracious, approachable, accessible, amenable, sociable, hail-fellow-well-met, outgoing, gregarious, neighborly.

antonyms: unfriendly.

Latin affabilis, from the verb affari, from ad- 'to' + fari 'speak.'

Activity: Explain the similarity of fable and affability.

equanimity

e·qua·nim·i·ty

Noun

ēkwəˈnimitē

mental calmness, composure, and evenness of temper, especially in a difficult situation.: "she accepted both the good and the bad with equanimity".

I was in awe of her equanimity under the duress we just endured.

synonyms: composure, calm, level-headedness, self-possession, coolheadedness, presence of mind.

antonyms: anxiety.

Latin aequanimitas, from aequus 'equal' + animus 'mind.' w/ even mind

Activity: equanimity is considered one of the four virtues of Buddhism, what are the other three?

precocious

pre·co·cious

Adjective

pri'kōSHəs

(of a child) having developed certain abilities or proclivities at an earlier age than usual.: "he was a precocious, solitary boy".

synonyms: advanced for one's age, forward, mature, gifted, talented, clever, intelligent, quick.

antonyms: backward.

Latin from praecoquere 'ripen fully,' from prae 'before' + coquere 'to cook') + -ious.

Activity: At what age is precocious puberty defined?

pedagogy

ped·a·go·gy

pedə͵gäjē

noun

the method and practice of teaching, especially as an academic subject or theoretical concept.

"the relationship between applied linguistics and language pedagogy"

Despite our success our pedagogical approach is outdated, I believe it would be more effective if we would approach it differently.

Greek paidagōgos, denoting a slave who accompanied a child to school (from pais, paid- 'boy' + agōgos 'guide').

idiosyncratic

id·i·o·syn·crat·ic

idēəsiNG'kratik

adjective

of or relating to idiosyncrasy; peculiar or individual.

"she emerged as one of the great idiosyncratic talents of the Nineties"

synonyms: distinctive, individual, individualistic, characteristic, peculiar, typical, special, specific, unique, one-of-a-kind, personal

Greek sunkratikos 'mixed together.'

HIs idiosyncracies of not being able to talk to women and Shyla's pathological shyness has somehow brought them together.

Activity: what is your unique idiosyncrasy?

winnow

win·now

winō

verb

remove (people or things) from a group until only the best ones are left.

"the contenders had been winnowed to five"

find or identify (a valuable or useful part of something).

"amidst this welter of confusing signals, it's difficult to winnow out the truth"

synonyms: separate (out), divide, segregate, sort out, sift out, filter out; isolate, narrow down; remove, get rid of

Do wino and wind come from the same word origin? How do they relate in meaning?

inconsonant

in·con·so·nant

Adjective

in'känsənənt

not in agreement or harmony; not compatible.

After reporting the incident, dealing with the government lead to inconsonant opinions of Alien life form.

What is the subtle difference in the origins of the words constant and consonant?

precept

pre·cept

Noun 'prē‚sept

precepts plural noun

a general rule intended to regulate behavior or thought.: "moral precepts" "the legal precept of being innocent until proven guilty" "children learn far more by example than by precept".

"Who stated "the precepts of the law are these: to live honestly, to injure no one and to give everyone else their due."

synonyms: principle, rule, tenet, canon, doctrine, command, order, decree, dictate, dictum, injunction, commandment.

Latin praecipere 'warn, instruct,'

Who stated "the precepts of the law are these: to live honestly, to injure no one and to give everyone else their due."?

conciliatory

con·cil·i·a·to·ry

Adjective

kənˈsilēəˌtôrē

intended or likely to placate or pacify.: "a conciliatory approach".

synonyms: propitiatory, placatory, appeasing, pacifying, mollifying, peacemaking.

penurious

pe·nu·ri·ous

pəˈn(y)o͞orēəs

adjective

extremely poor; poverty-stricken.

"a penurious old tramp"

synonyms: poor, poor as a church mouse, poverty-stricken, destitute, necessitous, impecunious, impoverished, indigent, needy, in need/want, badly off, in reduced/straitened circumstances, hard up, unable to make ends meet, penniless, without a cent (to one's name), without a sou; More

antonyms: wealthy

characterized by poverty or need.

"penurious years"

Latin penuria 'need, scarcity'

What is a common word used today that means penurious?

censures

cen·sure

senSHər

verb

the expression of formal disapproval.

"angry delegates offered a resolution of censure against the offenders"

synonyms: condemnation, criticism, attack, abuse

antonyms: approval

Latin = censura 'judgment, assessment,' from censere 'assess.'

delineates

de·lin·e·ate

Verb

di'linē‚āt

describe or portray (something) precisely.: "the law should delineate and prohibit behavior that is socially abhorrent".

synonyms: describe, set forth/out, present, outline, sketch, depict, represent.

Latin = delineat- 'outlined,'

aesthete

aes·thete

Noun

es‚THēt

a person who has or affects to have a special appreciation of art and beauty.

Greek aisthētēs 'a person who perceives'

pragmatic

prag·mat·ic

prag'matik

adjective

dealing with things sensibly and realistically in a way that is based on practical rather than theoretical considerations.

"a pragmatic approach to politics"

synonyms: practical, matter-of-fact, sensible, down-to-earth, commonsensical, businesslike, having both/one's feet on the ground, hard headed, no-nonsense; informal; hard-nosed
"she remains pragmatic in the most emotional circumstances"
antonyms: impractical
Latin from Greek pragmatikos 'relating to fact'
Compare/ Contrast the words : pragmatic and rash.

---

lithe

Adjective

līTH

(especially of a person's body) thin, supple, and graceful.

synonyms: agile, graceful, supple, limber, lithesome, loose-limbed, nimble, deft, flexible, lissome, slender, slim, willowy.

antonyms: clumsy.

German lind 'soft, gentle.'

How can you differentiate the word lithe and svelte? Give examples.

---

reprieve

re·prieve

Verb

ri'prēv

cancel or postpone the punishment of (someone, especially someone condemned to death).: "under the new regime, prisoners under sentence of death were reprieved".

synonyms: grant a stay of execution to, pardon, spare, grant an amnesty to, amnesty

How are the words "relief" and "reprieve" alike?

hubris

hu·bris

Noun ˈ(h)yo͞obris

hubris noun

excessive pride or self-confidence..

synonyms: arrogance, conceit, haughtiness, hauteur, pride, self-importance, egotism, pomposity, superciliousness, superiority.

antonyms: humility.

(in Greek tragedy) excessive pride toward or defiance of the gods, leading to nemesis.

Hubris was considered a crime in Ancient Greece, what was the punishment?

---

usurp

u·surp

Verb

yo͞oˈsərp

take (a position of power or importance) illegally or by force.: "Richard usurped the throne".

synonyms: seize, take over, take possession of, take, commandeer, wrest, assume, expropriate.

Latin = usurpare 'seize for use.'

---

obstinacy

ob·sti·na·cy

Noun

äbstənəsē

the quality or condition of being obstinate; stubbornness.: "his reputation for obstinacy".

synonyms: stubbornness, inflexibility, intransigence, intractability, obduracy, mulishness, pigheadedness, willfulness, contrariness, perversity, recalcitrance, refractoriness, implacability, rigidity, uncooperativeness.

antonyms: flexibility.

"The difference between perseverance and obstinacy is that one comes from a strong will, and the other from a strong won't."

Henry Ward Beecher

Which of the two words connote strong will?

impetuous

im·pet·u·ous

Adjective

im'peCHo͞oəs

acting or done quickly and without thought or care.: "her friend was headstrong and impetuous".

synonyms: impulsive, rash, hasty, overhasty, reckless, heedless, careless, foolhardy, bullheaded, headstrong, incautious, imprudent, injudicious, ill-considered, unthought-out.

antonyms: considered, cautious.

Latin = impetuosus, from impetere 'to assail, attack.'

What is the theory of impetus?

conjecture

con·jec·ture

kən'jekCHər

noun

an opinion or conclusion formed on the basis of incomplete information.

"conjectures about the newcomer were many and varied"

synonyms: speculation, guesswork, surmise, fancy, presumption, assumption, theory, postulation, supposition

antonyms: fact

Latin conjectura, from conicere 'put together in thought,' from con- 'together' + jacere 'throw.'

How does conjecture relates to the word hypothesis?

circumscribed

cir·cum·scribe

Verb

sərkəm͵skrīb

restrict (something) within limits.: "their movements were strictly monitored and circumscribed".

synonyms: restrict, limit, keep within bounds, curb, confine, restrain.

Latin = circumscribere, from circum 'around' + scribere 'write.'

How does circumference and circumscribe relate?

irreverent

ir·rev·er·ent

Adjective

iˈrev(ə)rənt

showing a lack of respect for people or things that are generally taken seriously.: "she is irreverent about the whole business of politics".

synonyms: disrespectful, disdainful, scornful, contemptuous, derisive, disparaging.

antonyms: respectful.

Latin irreverent- 'not revering,' from in- 'not' + reverent- 'revering'

corroborated

cor·rob·o·rate

Verb

kəˈräbəˌrāt

confirm or give support to (a statement, theory, or finding).: "the witness had corroborated the boy's account of the attack".

synonyms: confirm, verify, endorse, ratify, authenticate, validate, certify.

antonyms: contradict.

Latin corroborat- 'strengthened,' from the verb corroborare, from cor- 'together' + roborare, from robur 'strength.'

belied

be·lie

Verb

biˈlī

(of an appearance) fail to give a true notion or impression of (something); disguise or contradict.: "his lively alert manner belied his years".

synonyms: contradict, be at odds with, call into question, show/prove to be false, disprove, debunk, discredit, controvert, negate.

antonyms: testify to, reveal.

extant

ex·tant

Adjective ˈekstənt

extant adjective

(especially of a document) still in existence; surviving.: "the original manuscript is no longer extant".

synonyms: still existing, in existence, existent, surviving, remaining, undestroyed.

Latin exstant- 'being visible or prominent, existing,' from the verb exstare, from ex- 'out' + stare 'to stand.'

Compare & contrast the words extinct & extant?

---

tempered

Verb

serve as a neutralizing or counterbalancing force to (something). "their idealism is tempered with realism"

synonyms: moderate, modify, modulate, mitigate, alleviate, reduce, weaken, lighten, soften

"their idealism is tempered with realism"

Temper is a word used in cooking, how does tempered chocolate relate to the definition(s) above?

---

officious

of·fi·cious

əˈfiSHəs

adjective

assertive of authority in an annoyingly domineering way, especially with regard to petty or trivial matters.

"a policeman came to move them on, an officious, spiteful man"

synonyms: self-important, bumptious, self-assertive, overbearing, overzealous, domineering, opinionated, interfering, intrusive, meddlesome, meddling; More

antonyms: self-effacing

Latin officiosus 'obliging'

What is an officious intermeddler?

admonish

ad·mon·ish

ədˈmäniSH

verb

warn or reprimand someone firmly.

"she admonished me for appearing at breakfast unshaven"

synonyms: reprimand, rebuke, scold, reprove, reproach,

upbraid, chastise, chide, berate, criticize, take to task, read the riot

act to, rake/haul over the coals; More

advise or urge (someone) earnestly.

Latin admonere 'urge by warning.'

Can you contrast "admonish", "reprimand" and "censure",

imprudent

im·pru·dent

Adjective

imˈpro͞odnt

not showing care for the consequences of an action; rash.: "it

would be imprudent to leave her winter coat behind".

synonyms: unwise, injudicious, incautious, indiscreet, misguided,

ill-advised, ill-judged.

antonyms: sensible.

Latin imprudent- 'not foreseeing'

Having been imprudent in your past served you well? If so,

recount that experience.

denuded

de·nude

Verb

di'n(y)o͞od

strip (something) of its covering, possessions, or assets; make bare.: "almost overnight the Arctic was denuded of animals".

synonyms: strip, clear, deprive, bereave, rob.

antonyms: cover.

Latin denudare, from de- 'completely' + nudare 'to bare'

deliberation

de·lib·er·a·tion

Noun

di͜libə'rāSHən

long and careful consideration or discussion.: "after much deliberation, we arrived at a compromise" "the commission's deliberations".

synonyms: thought, consideration, reflection, contemplation, meditation, rumination.

Latin deliberatio(n-), from deliberare 'consider carefully'

Dilberate can also mean intentional. Can you make a sentence where you use both meanings?

amalgam

a·mal·gam

ə'malgəm

noun

a mixture or blend.

"a curious amalgam of the traditional and the modern"

Latin amalgama, from Greek malagma 'an emollient.'

Idiom Amalgamation is when you have a combination of two idioms. Can you make up your own?

fawning

fôn

verb

(of a person) give a servile display of exaggerated flattery or affection, typically in order to gain favor or advantage.

"congressmen fawn over the President"

synonyms: be obsequious to, be sycophantic to, curry favor with, flatter, play up to, crawl to, ingratiate oneself with, dance attendance on

The word fain and fawn come from the word :fagnian how are these words related?

obsequious

ob·se·qui·ous

Adjective

əbˈsēkwēəs

obedient or attentive to an excessive or servile degree.: "they were served by obsequious waiters".

synonyms: servile, ingratiating, sycophantic, fawning, unctuous, oily, oleaginous, groveling, cringing, subservient, submissive, slavish.

antonyms: domineering.

Latin obsequiosus, from obsequium 'compliance,' from obsequi 'follow, comply with.'

How does this word relate to the word obsequy? What does obsequy mean?

husbandry

management of resources

agriculture

synonyms: frugal thrift

antonyms: wastefulness

Recently moving the city lead to good husbandry, my loft alone was my whole paycheck!

_____ husbandry is the #1 in the world.

ignominious

marked by shame or disgrace, something/one who deserves shame, degrading

latin : ("loss of a good name, ignominy"), from *ig*- ("not") + *nomen* ("name")

Despite her best efforts to look good, her actions were ignominious at best.

antonyms: honorable, respectable

synonyms: disgraceful, dishonorable

What would be an ignominious act back in Ancient Rome?

smug- feeling of excessive pride in achievements or actions

Antonyms

Synonyms

Do smug and smuggle come from the same origin?

His smug face irritated me, his supposed achievements are nothing more than hot air.

nostalgia

nos·tal·gia

Nounnä'staljə

nostalgia noun;nostalgias plural noun

a sentimental longing or wistful affection for the past, typically for a

period or place with happy personal associations.

Listening to 90's music filled me such nostalgia I wasn't able to

hold back my tears.

synonym : homesick

antonym: _____

Hearing music from the early brought nostalgic thoughts to Mary,

feelings that she wasn't able to verbalize.

What food/candy brings about nostalgic thoughts?

countenance

demeanor

face

semblance

pretense

to support

latin - continens to contain

synonym: face

antonyms: to be against

His countenance paled in comparison to Steve's, Steve's support

for the cause came from the heart.

Explain how the word countenance would come from the root.

meaning to contain.

feigned- being fake

latin: fingere (mold, contrive)

synonyms: fake

antonyms: real

Her feigned smile was very obvious, she couldn't hide her disdain for the greasy food.

When was the last time you had to feign an emotion?

_____.

Manifesto

man·i·fes·to

a declaration of policies.

Latin: manifestus (obvious) → manifesto (make public)

synonyms:

The manifesto issued by the political party seemed very skewed. It didn't even touch upon the subjects we were hoping for.

synonyms

antonyms

What's the difference between the word creed and manifesto?

Use a sentence with the word manifesto as a verb.

_____.

prospectus : document that describes an institution or business and what they have to offer

latin: prospectus : view

synonyms: catalogue, syllabus

What does football prospectus contain?

arbitration-

arbitrari ("to arbitrate, judge)

process where two parties allow a third party to resolve a legal problem.

Synonym:

Antonym:

Before undergoing surgery, I had to watch an _____ video, the video stated that I was not able to sue for negligence or malpractice, instead it stated that if there was a problem it would be resolved via a third party.

Mandate- an official command

Latin : manus -hand + dare- to put

synonym :authorization

antonym:

The _mandate_ was not to leave the biohazard waste bins with open lids, it could lead to contamination of the atmosphere.

Can you explain what Mandate of Heaven is?

_____.

Remember to claim your FREE material!

Visit the following webpage and enter your email address to receive Flashcards of the Hardest Words plus bonus Vocabulary Games!

www.thesatmathprep.com/sat-vocab.html

Part 2

Vocabulary Practice

"There are only two types of people who will amount to nothing: those who will not do what they are told, and those who will do nothing else."
Napoleon Hill

Chapter 8: Fill in the Blanks Practice

All of the following problems are similar to difficulty level 5, the hardest questions on the . Remember if you're not sure of a vocabulary word, break down the word into the roots, then put together the roots to understand the meaning. In order to prepare to get the correct answer every time, let's familiarize ourselves with the wrong answer traps that the uses. The two most common wrong answer traps that the tries to trap you into are opposites and out of scope. The will commonly use answers with vocab words that are antonyms of what you want to pick, or mean something completely different. He is some practice, and answers and explanations follow, with correct answers in bold.

1. Many of his close friends call Mike's behavior _____, his impulsive nature and ever changing whims giving rise to the label.

(A) benign   (B) influential   (C) capricious

(D) stealthy   (E) loquacious

2. The idea of building an addition to his house became _____ as a result of _____, the plans to create more space stagnated by the rigid policies of the township's board.

(A) hastened . . infighting   (B) blunted . . jingoism
(C) ossified . . bureaucratization   (D) ostracized . . invention
(E) revered . . legislation

3. My friend is incapable of hiding her _____ smile when she sees the beggar on the street, as if saying that she is so much better off than him.

(A) humble   (B) deferential   (C) supercilious
        (D) infectious   (E) candid

4. There are many unspoken _____ that we have to adhere to if we don't want to get fired.

(A) dictums   (B) recourse   (C) transgressions
        (D) secrets   (E) arrhythmias

5. While trying to get straight answers from the insurance company as to why my child's care wasn't paid for, I was completely dismayed in trying to understand their _____ insurance regulations.

(A) intelligible   (B) unambiguous   (C) comprehensible
        (D) feign   (E) byzantine

6. The football analyst was often lauded for his football _____: his keen judgment and insightful decisions were widely acknowledged.

(A) acumen   (B) denseness   (C) obtuseness
        (D) ineptness   (E) etiquette

7. Because the business owner generously donated to the politicians running for local office, they remembered this _____ and returned the favor when he needed one.

(A) incompatibility   (B) animosity   (C) subterfuge

         (D) magnanimity   (E) patronage

8. The class-clown would persistently badger the teacher with _____ questions, the absurdity causing a stir among the rest of the class.

(A) ingenious   (B) intelligent   (C) inane

         (D) esoteric   (E) enigmatic

9. The _____ land has been fiercely fought over by the two religions for the past 60 years, both claiming that they are entitled to its inheritance by divine right.

(A) condemned   (B) depreciated   (C) futile

         (D) cursed   (E) consecrate

10. Job losses are the unfortunate _____ of budget cutting.

(A) beginning   (B) cause   (C) corollary

         (D) commencement   (E) surplus

11. He was _____ the death of his infant daughter, his grief could not be consoled for the first six months.

(A) lamenting   (B) lauding   (C) relieving
     (D) laboring   (E) proselytizing

12. The research has been carried out with _____ attention to detail

(A) scrupulous   (B) careless   (C) undemanding
     (D) unassuming   (E) scintillating

13. His knowledge of French, Italian, and Spanish made him genuinely _____

(A) unsophisticated   (B) cosmopolitan   (C) unrefined
     (D) mundane   (E) consecrated

14. The elder officer refused to tolerate any backtalk from his _____ officers.

(A) superior   (B) chief   (C) incommensurate
     (D) subordinate   (E) unwieldy

15. Everything was as it would have appeared in centuries past apart from one _____, a bright yellow modern construction crane.

(A) boon   (B) anachronism   (C) attainment
     (D) windfall   (E) synchronicity

16. The careless manager caused many problems with his _____ management.

(A) meticulous   (B) polished   (C) slipshod
    (D) orderly   (E) immaculate

17. Critics of the administration _____ the president for his failure to tackle the deficiency.

(A) exonerated   (B) commended   (C) reproached
    (D) lauded   (E) subjugated

18. The weaker army used a relatively _____, homemade bomb, while the stronger army used sophisticated drones to win the war.

(A) planned   (B) polished   (C) cumbersome
    (D) egregious   (E) crude

19. She thought the teacher was arrogant and _____, patronizing her learning deficiencies at every opportunity.

(A) condescending   (B) friendly   (C) reassuring
    (D) protagonist   (E) conjugating

20. The actress looked the _____ of elegance and good taste, wearing a champagne color dress and diamond studded necklace on the red carpet.

(A) abridgement   (B) extension   (C) annexation
    (D) epitome   (E) antithesis

Answers & Explanations

1. We're looking for a word here that means "impulsive, ever changing." Benign means harmless. Influential means persuasive. **Capricious means sudden and unaccountable changes of mood, so our best answer is (C) Capricious.** Stealthy means sneaking or sly. Loquacious means excessively talkative. All answers except for C are out of scope.

2. In this problem, we are looking for two words that are defined towards the second half of the sentence. We need to identify a word that means "stagnated" in the first blank, and one that means "rigid policies" in the second blank. Hastened means rushed, which is the opposite of what we're looking for, and infighting refers to conflict within an organization, which is out of scope. Blunted means dull, and jingoism means extreme patriotism, both out of scope. **(C) Ossified and Bureaucratization mean exactly what we are looking for.** Ostracized means to exclude, and invention means creation, which are both out of scope. Revered means respect, which is out of scope and legislation means rulings. Legislation may loosely work, but revered does not work at all, therefore E is incorrect.

3. Here we are to identify a word that means arrogant. Humble is the opposite, as is deferential. **(C) Supercilious is the answer we are looking for**, while infectious and candid are both out of scope.

4. **(A) Dictums is the correct answer because we're looking for a word here which means informal order or rule set by an authority.** Recourse doesn't fit, because that means 'a source of help out of a difficult situation.' Transgressions are wrongdoings, so that won't work. Secrets can be unspoken, but don't let that throw you off… we don't have to adhere to secrets to prevent getting fired. Arrhythmias are completely out of scope - that is a medical condition in which the heart beats irregularly.

5. This one may not be entirely clear at first. Some questions on the are best tackled by process of elimination. You should also recognize that the correct answer should be a word that deals with administrative complexities. Let's go word by word to see if we can eliminate any options. Intelligible means understandable, so we can eliminate that. Unambiguous means clear, which is the opposite of what we're looking for, so we can eliminate that. Comprehensible also means understandable, so that can be eliminated. Feign means to fake, so that can also be eliminated. **The correct answer is (E) Byzantine, which means excessively complicated and involving a great deal of administrative detail. Definitely correct.**

6. We're looking for a word here which means keen judgment and insightful decisions. **(A) Acumen fits in the space perfectly.** Denseness is the opposite, meaning mentally slow and limited as does obtuseness. Ineptness means awkward and lacking skill. Etiquette refers to manners.

7. We're looking for a word that means generously donated. Incompatibility refers to incapability in existing together. Animosity refers to hostility. Subterfuge refers to trickery. **(D) magnanimity is the correct answer because magnanimity refers to generosity.** Patronage is a sponsor, backer or financier.

8. We are looking for a word that means absurd. Ingenious means clever, original, and inventive. Intelligent refers to smarts or brilliance. Both of those first two options are out of scope. **(C) inane is the correct answer, meaning silly or absurd.** Esoteric means obscure, and enigmatic means mysterious, both of which are out of scope.

9. We're looking for a word here that means holy, and our clue was the words divine right, indicating some sort of higher power has given the land. Condemned is an opposite of what we're looking for, as it means disapproved. Depreciated refers to a loss in value. Futile means pointless, vain, or useless. Cursed again, is the opposite of what we're looking for, meaning doomed. **(E) consecrated is the correct answer, meaning to make or declare something sacred.**

10. We want to fill in a word here that basically means "follows as a result of something that came before it." Beginning, cause, and commencement are all opposites of that which we're looking for. **(C) corollary means exactly what we were looking for.** Surplus means an excess of, or oversupply, and that's completely out of scope for our problem.

11. **The correct answer choice here is the word that means mourning, and the correct answer is (A) lamenting.** Lauding means praise, and is the opposite of what we're looking for. Relieving is out of scope, and means to cause to become less severe. Laboring means to work hard. Proselytizing means attempting to convert people to another religion or ideas.

12. **We need an answer here that means, extremely careful, and (A) scrupulous fits best because scrupulous means diligent, thorough, and extremely attentive to detail.** Careless is the opposite of what we're looking for. Undemanding means easy, unassuming means modest, and scintillating means sparkling, or shining brightly -- all three words are out of scope.

13. The clues of this sentence are that the person is familiar with three different languages. That is a sophisticated attribute, so answer choice (A) unsophisticated would be the opposite. **(B) cosmopolitan means to be comfortable with different countries and cultures, so this would be a perfect fit.** Unrefined means crude or unfinished. Mundane means boring. Consecrated means made or declared something as sacred.

14. It's generally unacceptable in hierarchical systems like the police force for a lower ranking officer to talk back to a higher ranking official, so we're looking for a word which means lower in rank. Superior is the opposite and means above in rank, as does chief. Incommensurate means not in proportion with. **(D) subordinate is the correct answer we are looking for, and the definition is lower in rank or position.** Unwieldy means difficult to carry due to its size, shape, or weight.

15. We're looking for a word that means out of place and belonging to a different time period. Boon is a blessing, and that's totally out of scope. **(B) anachronism is exactly right, that means a thing belonging to or appropriate to a period other than that which it exists.** Attainment means achieving a goal that one has worked towards. Windfall is a fruit blown down from a tree by the wind. Synchronicity is the simultaneous occurrence of events.

16. We're looking for the word which means careless. Meticulous means extremely careful, which is the opposite. Polished has more than one definition, and can mean shiny or refined. **(C) slipshod is the correct answer because slipshod means characterized by a lack of care, thought or organization.** Orderly, means neat and methodically arranged, while immaculate means perfectly clean, neat or tidy. Both (D) and (E) are opposites of what we are looking for.

17. Critics normally express disappointment and negativity towards who or what the critics are criticizing. Therefore, (A), (B), and (D) would be incorrect because all are opposites that have a positively charged connotation. **(C) reproached is the correct answer, which means to address with expressed disapproval or disappointment.** Subjugated means bring under control or domination, especially by conquest, and this answer is out of scope.

18. The word we're looking for here has to match the simplistic, rudimentary nature of homemade technology. Planned and polished seem to be the opposite of what we need. Cumbersome means large or heavy and is out of scope. Egregious means terrible or awful is also out of scope. (E) crude is our best answer meaning exactly primitive, simplistic, and basic.

19. For this answer, we need a word that means patronizing by a person in power. **(A) condescending fits well meaning patronizing, supercilious, or snobby, and is the best answer choice.** Let's see why the other answer choices don't make sense. (B), (C), and (D) are all opposites. Conjugated means being combined with.

20. We need to find a word here that means personification or embodiment. Abridgement is a shortened version, and extension is an addition. Annexation is a seizure or occupation. So far, (A), (B), and (C) are out of scope. **(D) epitome fits perfectly, and that's our best answer, meaning a person or thing that is a perfect example of a particular quality or type.** Antithesis means converse or contrary, and this option is the opposite of what we are looking for.

Chapter 9: Short Passages Practice

This passage, about psychologist Sigmund Freud's approach to dream study, was adapted from a beginners book on dream psychology.

1   The medical profession is justly conservative. Human life should not be considered as the proper material for wild experiments. Conservatism, however, is too often a welcome excuse for lazy minds, loath to adapt themselves to fast changing 5 conditions. Remember the scornful reception which first was accorded to Freud's discoveries in the domain of the unconscious.

When after years of patient observations, he finally decided to appear before medical bodies to tell them modestly of some facts which always recurred in his dream and his patients' dreams, 10 he was first laughed at and then avoided as a crank.

The words "dream interpretation" were and still are indeed fraught with unpleasant, unscientific associations. They remind one of all sorts of childish, superstitious notions, which make up the thread and woof of dream books, read by none but the 15 ignorant and the primitive.

The wealth of detail, the infinite care never to let anything pass unexplained, with which he presented to the public the result of his investigations, are impressing more and more serious-minded scientists, but the examination of his evidential data 20 demands arduous work and presupposes an absolutely open mind.

This is why we still encounter men, totally unfamiliar with Freud's writings, men who were not even interested enough in the subject to attempt an interpretation of their dreams or their
25 patients' dreams, deriding Freud's theories and combatting them with the help of statements which he never made.

Some of them, like Professor Boris Sidis, reach at times conclusions which are strangely similar to Freud's, but in their ignorance of psychoanalytic literature, they fail to credit Freud for
30 observations antedating theirs.

Besides those who sneer at dream study, because they have never looked into the subject, there are those who do not dare to face the facts revealed by dream study. Dreams tell us many an unpleasant biological truth about ourselves and only very
35 free minds can thrive on such a diet. Self-deception is a plant which withers fast in the pellucid atmosphere of dream investigation. The neurotic attached to his neurosis is not anxious to turn such a powerful searchlight upon the dark corners of their psychology.
40 Freud's theories are anything but theoretical. He was moved by the fact that there always seemed to be a close connection between his patients' dreams and their mental abnormalities, to collect thousands of dreams and to compare them with the case histories in his possession.
45 He did not start out with a preconceived bias, hoping to find evidence which might support his views. He looked at facts a thousand times "until they began to tell him something." His attitude toward dream study was, in other words, that of a statistician who does not know, and has no means of foreseeing,

50 what conclusions will be forced on him by the information he is gathering, but who is fully prepared to accept those inexorable conclusions.

1. In line 2, "loath" most nearly means

(A) inclined   (B) unwilling   (C) disposed

(D) ungrudging   (E) volunteering

2. In line 3, "scornful" most nearly means

(A) reverential   (B) deferential   (C) gracious

(D) biddable   (E) contemptuous

3. In line 17, "deriding" most nearly means

(A) ridicule   (B) exalt   (C) eulogize

(D) venerate   (E) lionize

4. In line 20, "antedating" most nearly means

(A) emanate   (B) ensue   (C) precede

(D) mimic   (E) intimate

5. In line 24, "pellucid" most nearly means

(A) clear   (B) opaque   (C) smeary

(D) cloudy   (E) incomprehensible

6. In line 24, "neurotic" most nearly means

(A) balanced   (B) mature   (C) unstable

(D) sensible   (E) practical

7. In line 32, "forced on him" most nearly means

(A) Freud forcefully argued his own views on dream theory despite the data telling him the contrary

(B) The information was inaccurate yet he was forced to accept it for fear of persecution

(C) Freud was a statistician driven by preconceived notions and bias

(D) The statistical analysis of patient's information was so compelling that it has to be accepted as truth

(E) Although ahead of his time, society ridiculed Freud and made him recant his position on dreams

8. In line 33, "inexorable" probably means

(A) unavoidable   (B) preventable   (C) inexplicable

(D) unfathomable   (E) rousing

Answers & Explanations

1. From what we know about conservatism, conservatives tend to hold on to traditions of the past and are not willing to embrace change, if at ever all. Inclined, disposed, ungrudging, and volunteering all mean a form of willing, so all do not fit. **(B) unwilling fits best because loath means unwilling.**

2. Scornful has a strong negative connotation. By knowing this, we could eliminate (A), (B), and (C) as those all have positive connotations: highly esteemed, respected, and grateful, respectively. Biddable means cooperative. **All of those previous choices are the opposites of the correct answer, which is (E) contemptuous.**

3. We're looking for a word with a strong negative connotation here, as the author laces this entire passage with illustrations and examples of how negatively and closed mindedly people received Freud's work. **(A) ridicule fits best as the men the author talks about expressed contempt for, or ridiculed, Freud strongly.** The other choices, exalt, eulogize, venerate, and lionize all have positive connotations which mean public praise. This is the opposite of what Freud received initially for his work.

4. The author says here that other scientists came to conclusions strikingly similar to Freud's work, and even though Freud's work came before theirs, those scientists did not give Freud credit for his influence or his work. (A) emanate means originate from, and this is the opposite. (B) ensue means result from, **(C) precede is the best answer because it means came before, and that implies that Freud's work came before the other scientist's work.** (D) mimic means imitate, and Freud didn't imitate the work of those scientists. (E) intimate means close or familiar to, and this is out of scope. The best way to answer this is to look at the Latin prefix ANTE- and see that it means, come before.

5. **Based on this paragraph, the author insinuates that dreams provide clear truth even for those who have a false sense of reality while awake and alert, so (A) clear, is the best answer.** All of the other answer choices mean the opposite. Opaque means nontransparent, smeary means marked by smears, cloudy means nontransparent as well, and incomprehensible means unclear.

6. Neurotic means mentally ill, or unstable mentally. Balanced and mature mean the opposite of what we are looking for. **(C) unstable is the best answer and fits the definition of neurotic here.** Sensible and practical are also the opposite of neurotic.

7. The wording of this sentence using 'forced on him' implied that Freud had to accept the data as truth because he worked so hard to compile the data from hundreds of patients. The passage entirely supports Freud, and this sentence belabors the point of how true Freud's work was, based on the scientific method and statistical analysis. (A) is incorrect because Freud did not force his views, instead his views came to him from analyzing data objectively. (B) is incorrect because the passage says nothing about the data being inaccurate. (C) Although it's true Freud was a statistician in a way, he did not have preconceived notions or bias. **(D) The statistical analysis of patient's information was so compelling that it has to be accepted as truth is the best answer.** (E) is incorrect because this is out of scope and does not answer this question, although it is true.

8. **Inexorable means inevitable, or unavoidable, therefore (A) unavoidable is the best answer.** Freud had no preconceived notions or bias about the results of the statistical analysis. Instead, he accept the unavoidable truth presented to him by the process. Preventable does not fit, and inexplicable means unexplainable as does unfathomable. Rousing means exciting or inspiring, and this is out of scope.

Chapter 10: Long Passages Practice

Questions 1-8 are based on the following passage.

The following passage has been adapted from Myths and Marvels of Astronomy written by Richard A. Proctor in 1896.

1   The belief must have been all but universal in those days that at the birth of any person who was to hold an important place in the world's history the stars would either be ominously conjoined, or else some blazing comet or new star would make its 5 appearance. For we know that some such object having appeared, or some unusual conjunction of planets having occurred, near enough to the time of Christ's birth to be associated in men's minds with that event, it came eventually to be regarded as belonging to his horoscope, and as actually indicating to the
10 Wise Men of the East the future greatness of the child then born. It is certain that that is what the story of the Star in the East means as it stands. Theologians differ as to its interpretation in points of detail. Some think the phenomenon was meteoric, others that a comet then made its appearance, others that a new star
15 shone out, and others that the account referred to a conjunction of Jupiter, Saturn, and Mars, which occurred at about that time. As a matter of detail it may be mentioned, that none of these explanations in the slightest degree corresponds with the account, for neither meteor, nor comet, nor new star, nor conjoined 20 planets, would go before travelers from the east, to show them their way to any place. Yet the ancients sometimes regarded comets as guides. Whichever view we accept, it is abundantly clear that an

astrological significance was attached by the narrator to the event. And not so very long ago, when astrologers first

25 began to see that their occupation was passing from them, the Wise Men of the East were appealed to against the enemies of astrology—very much as Moses was appealed to against Copernicus and Galileo, and more recently to protect us against certain relationships which Darwin, Wallace, and Huxley unkindly 30 indicate for the human race divine.

Although astronomers now reject altogether the doctrines of judicial astrology, it is impossible for the true lover of that science to regard astrology altogether with contempt. Astronomy, indeed, owes much more to the notions of believers in astrology 35 than is commonly supposed. Astrology bears the same relation to modern astronomy that alchemy bears to modern chemistry. As it is probable that nothing but the hope of gain, literally in this case *auri sacra fames*, would have led to those laborious researches of the alchemists which first taught men how to analyze matter into its 40 elementary constituents, and afterwards to combine

these constituents afresh into new forms, so the belief that, by carefully studying the stars, men might acquire the power of predicting future events, first directed attention to the movements of the celestial bodies. Kepler's saying, that astrology, though a

45 fool, was the daughter of a wise mother, does not by any means present truly the relationship between astrology and astronomy. Rather we may say that astrology and alchemy, though foolish mothers, gave birth to those wise daughters, astronomy and chemistry. Even this way of speaking scarcely does justice to 50 the astrologers and alchemists of old times. Their views appear foolish in the light of modern scientific knowledge, but they were not foolish

in relation to what was known when they were entertained. Modern analysis goes far to demonstrate the immutability, and, consequently, the non-transmutability of the

55 metals, though it is by no means so certain as many suppose that the present position of the metals in the list of *elements* is really correct. Certainly a chemist of our day would be thought very unwise who should undertake a series of researches with the object of discovering a mineral having such qualities as the

60 alchemists attributed to the philosopher's stone. But when as yet the facts on which the science of chemistry is based were unknown, there was nothing unreasonable in supposing that such a mineral might exist, or the means of compounding it be discovered. Nay, many arguments from analogy might be urged to 65 show that the supposition was altogether probable. In like

manner, though the known facts of astronomy oppose themselves irresistibly to any belief in planetary influences upon the fates of men and nations, yet before those facts were discovered it was not only not unreasonable, but was in fact, highly reasonable to

70 believe in such influences, or at least that the sun, and moon, and stars moved in the heavens in such sort as to indicate what would happen. If the wise men of old times rejected the belief that 'the stars in their courses fought for or against men, they yet could not very readily abandon the belief that the stars were for signs in

75 the heavens of what was to befall mankind.

1. In line 2, "ominously" most nearly means

(A) auspiciously   (B) apocalyptic   (C) promisingly
    (D) favorably   (E) propitiously

2. In line 4, "conjunction" most nearly means

(A) antagonism   (B) detachment   (C) separation
    (D) coincidence   (E) division

3. In line 8, "phenomenon" most nearly means

(A) anomaly   (B) usualness   (C) regularity
    (D) normality   (E) audaciousness

4. In line 19, "judicial" most nearly means

(A) administrative   (B) criminal   (C) malefactor
    (D) illegal   (E) delinquent

5. In line 23, "laborious" most nearly means

(A) uncomplicated   (B) elementary   (C) arduous
    (D) facile   (E) monotonous

6. In line 30, "scarcely" most nearly means

(A) abundantly   (B) plentifully   (C) barely
    (D) effortlessly   (E) startlingly

7. In line 33, "non-transmutability" most nearly means

(A) metamorphose   (B) adaptability   (C)   transformation
    (D) consistent   (E) non-permanent

8. In line 39, "supposition" most nearly means

(A) belief   (B) indecision   (C) incertitude
    (D) riskiness   (E) caprice

Answers and Explanations

1. **The Latin suffix ominosus means evil omen, which most nearly matches with the best answer choice, (B) apocalyptic.** The author writes about an event happening in the stars conjunction with the birth of a historically significant person, which may seem like an unreal, earth shaking event. Also, the other answer choices are very similar to each other in meaning, and they are all the opposite of the correct answer choice. Auspiciously, promisingly, favorably, and propitiously all mean "indicating a good chance of success."

2. Recall that Latin base word jung means to join. The word conjunction therefore, means two events of things coming together at the same point in time or space. **Answer choice (D) coincidence is your best answer.** All of the other answer choices imply some division or separation, meaning the opposite of what we are looking for. Antagonism means hostility, detachment, separation, and division all imply some form of separation, not joining together.

3. A phenomenon is a fact or situation that is observed to exist or happen, especially one whose cause or explanation is in question. **(A) anomaly is the best answer, as anomaly means a deviation from what is normal or expected.** Usualness, regularity, normality, and audaciousness are all opposites to the best answer.

4. The Latin based word judic means judge or judgment. **Judicial, therefore, refers to legal administration. (A) administrative is the best answer choice.** All other answers, criminal (crimin), malefactor (male), illegal (il), and delinquent all mean the opposite of what we are looking for. Roots you should recognize are parenthesized.

5. Latin base word labor means work, exertion. **(C) arduous is the only answer choice which means to be on fire, to burn as in from over exertion.** Uncomplicated, elementary, and facile all mean simple, basic, or easy. Monotonous means boring or uninteresting.

6. Scarcity means only just, almost not enough. Abundantly and plentifully mean the opposite, while **(C) barely is the best answer.** Effortlessly means easily, and startlingly means surprisingly.

7. Non means not, and transmutability means changeability. Non-transmutability, therefore, means non-changeable, or consistent. Answer choices, (A), (B), (C), and (E) and incorrect because those all refer to the opposite. **(D) consistent matches what we are looking for, therefore this is the correct answer choice.**

8. Latin base word supponere means to suppose, and this is the origin of the word supposition. **Answer choice (A) belief, is the best fit here.** Indecision means inability to make a decision quickly and incertitude means a state of uncertainty, both opposites. Riskiness means full of the possibility of danger, which is out of scope, as is caprice which is a sudden and unaccountable change of behavior.

Questions 1-12 are based on the following passage.

The following passage has been adapted from Modern Marriage and How to Bear it, by Maud Churton Braby.

1 'Why women don't marry? But they do—whenever they can!' the intelligent reader will naturally exclaim. Not 'whenever they get the chance,' mark you; no *intelligent* reader would make this mistake, though it is a common enough error among the non-
5 comprehending. Most spinsters over thirty must have winced at one time or another at the would-be genial rallying of some elderly

man relative: 'What! you not married yet?

Well, well, I wonder what all the young men are thinking of.'
I write *some man* advisedly, for no woman, however cattishly
10 inclined, however desirous of planting arrows in a rival's breast,
would utter this peculiarly deadly form of insult, which, strangely
enough, is always intended as a high compliment by the masculine
blunderer. The fact that the unfortunate spinster thus assailed may
have had a dozen offers, and yet, for reasons of her own, prefer to
15 remain single, seems entirely beyond their range of
comprehension.

But the main reason why women don't marry is obviously
because men don't ask them. Most women will accept when a
sufficiently pleasing man offers them a sufficiently congenial life. If
20 the offers they receive fall below a certain standard, then they
prefer to remain single, wistfully hoping, no doubt, that the right man
may come along before it is too late. The preservation of the
imaginative faculty in women, to which I have previously alluded,
doubtless accounts for many spinsters. It must also be
25 remembered that the more educated women become, the less
likely they are to marry for marrying's sake as their grandmothers
did.

Then there are a few women, quite a small section, who,
unless they can realize their ideal in its entirety, will not be content
30 with second best. By an irony of fate, it happens that these are
often the noblest of their sex. Yet another small section remain
single from an honest dislike of marriage and its duties. It is
perhaps not too severe to say that a woman who has absolutely no
vocation for wifehood and motherhood must be a degenerate, and
35 so lacking in the best feminine instincts as to deserve the

reproach of being 'sexless.' This type is apparently increasing! I shall deal with it further in Part IV.

Then there are those—I should not like to make a guess at their number—who will marry *any* man, however undesirable and
40 uncongenial, rather than be left 'withering on the stalk.' It is an acutely humiliating fact that there exists no man too ugly, too foolish, too brutal, too conceited and too vile to find a wife. *Any* man can find *some* woman to wed him. In this connection, one recalls the famous cook, who, when condoled with on the defection 45 of a lover, replied: 'It don't matter; thank God I can love any man!'

One cannot help being amused by the serious articles on this subject in feminine journals. We are gravely told that women don't marry nowadays because they price their liberty too high,
50 because those who have money prefer to be independent and enjoy life, and those who have none prefer bravely wringing a living from the world to being a man's slave, a mere drudge, entirely engrossed in housekeeping, etc., etc.; and so on—pages of it! All this may possibly be true of a very small portion of the
55 community, but the incontrovertible fact remains that the principal reason for woman's spinsterhood is man's indifference.

1. In line 2, "mark" most nearly means

(A) obscured   (B) neglect   (C) disregard
        (D) discolor   (E) heed

2. In line 3, "winced" most nearly means

(A) beamed   (B) twinkled   (C) grinned

(D) grimaced   (C) cried

3. In line 4, "genial" most nearly means

(A) affable   (B) antagonistic   (C) aggressive
              (D) hostile   (E) youthful

4. In line 8, "blunder" most nearly means

(A) mistake   (B) chauvinist   (C) brute
              (D) jingoist   (E) joker

5. In line 8, "assailed" most nearly means

(A) protected   (B) guarded   (C) secured
              (D) shielded   (E) attacked

6. In line 11, "congenial" most nearly means

(A) unpleasant   (B) displeasing   (C) repugnant
              (D) repulsive   (E) hospitable

7. In line 13, "faculty" most nearly means

(A) impotence   (B) power   (C) inability
              (D) incapability   (E) incapacity

8. In line 21, "degenerate" most nearly means

(A) upstanding   (B) decent   (C) noble

    (D) dishonorable   (E) scrupulous

9. In line 21, "reproach" most nearly means

(A) approval   (B) commendation   (C) exoneration

    (D) disgrace   (E) sanction

10. In line 24, "acutely" most nearly means

(A) slightly   (B) moderately   (C) extremely

    (D) faintly   (E) vaguely

11. In line 30, "wringing" most nearly means

(A) pontificating   (B) intubating   (C) twisting

    (D) insinuating   (E) strangling

12. In line 33, "incontrovertible" most nearly means

(A) questionable   (B) indisputable   (C) contentious

    (D) doubtful   (E) dubious

Answers & Explanations

1. **Mark in this context means "mark my word", or (E) heed, which is the correct answer.** Mark can also mean obscured or discolored, but not in this context. Neglect and disregard are opposites of heed.

2. **Wince is a grimace caused by fear or distress, therefore (D) grimace is the best answer choice.** (A), (B), and (C), all have positive connotations, and wince has a negative connotation, so we can eliminate all of these choices. (D) Cried, is too extreme and does not mean wince either.

3. The Latin word genialis means of birth, generation, conducive to growth. **This came to mean joyful and conducive to growth of friendship, which makes (A) affable the best answer choice.**

4. **A blunder is a careless mistake, therefore (A) mistake is the best answer choice.** A chauvinist shows excessive loyalty to a particular cause. Brute is a savage, a jingoist is patriotism in the form of excessive foreign policy, and a joker is a comedian. The can all be eliminated.

5. Answer choices (A), (B), (C), and (D) all show the opposite meaning of assailed. **(E) attack is the best answer, as assailed means make a concerted or violent attack on.**

6. **The Latin root genial was used most commonly in the late 1800s, and again here, the root is in the word congenial, which in this case means (E) hospitable.** This is similar to friendly or affable in questions #3. The opposites of congenial are in answer choices (A), (B), (C), and (D) and are meant to trap you.

7. **Faculty means an inherent mental or physical power, therefore (B) power is the correct answer choice.** Impotence, inability, incapability, and incapacity are all opposites of the correct meaning of faculty.

8. Degenerate means having lost the mental, physical, or moral qualities considered normal and desirable. **The correct answer choice is (D) dishonorable.** Upstanding means honest, respectable, which is the opposite, as does decent. Noble is the extreme opposite, while scrupulous means paying close attention to detail. This is out of scope.

9. **Reproach means to address in such a way as to express disapproval or disappointment, and out of the answer choices, (D) disgrace is the best answer choice here.** Answer choices (A), (B), (C), and (E) are all opposites.

10. The Latin base word acurer means to sharpen, and acute means intense or severe. Think of acute pain as a bee sting being extremely intense, sharp pain. (A), (B), and (D) mean the opposite while (E) is out of scope. **Therefore, (C) extremely is the best answer.**

11. Wringing means squeezing and twisting to force liquid out. (A) pontificating is out of scope, meaning to preach. (B) intubating is also out of scope meaning to insert a tube into. (D) insinuating is out of scope as well, meaning to imply. (E) strangling means to choke, which may be related to twisting, but is not the best answer. **(C) twisting is the best answer to define wringing.**

12. Incontrovertible means not able to be denied or disputed, as the Latin word contra means against, and putting the prefixes and suffixes together we have, 'not able to go against'. (A) questionable is the opposite. (C) contentious means disputable, and is also the opposite, as is (D) doubtful and (E) dubious. **The correct answer is (B) indisputable, meaning unable to be challenged or denied.**

Part 3
Vocabulary Games

"Nothing can be called failure until you accept it as such."
Napoleon Hill

Chapter 11: Vocabulary Crossword Puzzles

Complete Crossword #1 below.

Across

1. Relating to the business of running an organization, or government.

2. Not friendly or forthcoming; cool and distant

3. Tending to talk a great deal; talkative.

Down

1. Given to sudden and unaccountable changes of mood or behavior
2. A plan or scheme, especially one used to outwit an opponent or achieve an end
3. Extreme patriotism, especially in the form of aggressive or warlike foreign policy
4. A person's social environment
5. Hold or express opinions that are at variance with those previously, commonly, or officially expressed
6. Looking or sounding sad and dismal
7. A formal pronouncement from an authoritative source, important idea or rule
8. In keeping with good taste and propriety; polite and restrained, honor

Word Bank

Stratagem
Dictum
Milieu
Aloof
Bureaucratization
Capricious
Loquacious
Decorous
Lugubrious
Dissent
Jingoism

Key #1

Across

1. bureaucratization
2. aloof
3. loquacious

Down

1. capricious
2. stratagem
3. jingoism
4. milieu
5. dissent
6. lugubrious
7. dictum
8. decorous

Complete Crossword #2 below.

Across

1. The use of many words where fewer would do, especially in a deliberate attempt to be vague or evasive.

2. Many and of various types.

3. Clever or cunning devices or expedients, especially as used to trick or deceive others.

Down

1. regard or represent as being of little worth
2. split or crack (something) to form a long narrow opening
3. characterized by or appealing to an abnormal and unhealthy interest in disturbing and unpleasant subjects, especially death and disease
4. adroitness and sensitivity in dealing with others or with difficult issues
5. a thing belonging or appropriate to a period other than that in which it exists, especially a thing that is conspicuously old-fashioned
6. clever or skillful in using the hands or mind
7. wicked or criminal
8. the use of fallacious arguments, especially with the intention of deceiving.
9. the ability to make good judgments and quick decisions, typically in a particular domain
10. expressed clearly; easy to understand

Word Bank

Artifice

Lucid

Circumlocutions

Disparage

Multifarious

Acumen

Sophistry

Nefarious

Fissure

Adroit

Morbid

Anachronism

Tactful

Key #2

Across

1. circumlocutions
2. multifarious
3. artifice

Down

1. disparage
2. fissure
3. morbid
4. tactful
5. anachronism
6. adroit
7. nefarious
8. sophistry
9. acumen
10. lucid

Complete Crossword #3 below.

Across

1. the use of many words where fewer would do, especially in a deliberate attempt to be vague or evasive.
2. familiar with and at ease in many different countries and cultures.
3. complain or find fault continually, typically about trivial matters.
4. (typically of an action or activity) wicked or criminal.
5. made in an intricate shape or decorated with complex patterns.

Down

1. dealing with things sensibly and realistically in a way that is based on practical rather than theoretical considerations.
2. (especially of a person's body) thin, supple, and graceful.
3. acting or done quickly and without thought or care
4. an opinion or conclusion formed on the basis of incomplete information.
5. give a servile display of exaggerated flattery or affection, typically in order to gain favor or advantage.
6. an official command
7. many and of various types.
8. shorten (something) by cutting off the top or the end.

Word Bank

Truncate

Mandate

Conjecture

Lithe

Ornate

Carp

Circumlocutions

Cosmopolitan

Nefarious

Pragmatic

Impetuous

Fawning

multifarious

Key #3

Across

circumlocutions

cosmopolitan

carp

nefarious

ornate

Down

pragmatic

lithe

impetuous

conjecture

fawning

mandate

multifarious

truncate

Key #3

Across

circumlocutions

cosmopolitan

carp

nefarious

ornate

Down

pragmatic

lithe

impetuous

conjecture

fawning

mandate

multifarious

truncate

ACTIONS TO COMPLETE AFTER YOU HAVE READ THIS BOOK

1. Review this book

If this book helped you, please post your positive feedback on the site you purchased it from; e.g. Amazon, Barnes and Noble, etc.

2. Claim your FREE bonuses

If you have not done so yet, visit the following webpage and enter your email address to receive Bonus Flashcards of the Hardest Words, plus more Vocabulary Games!

www.thesatmathprep.com/sat-vocab.html

About the Authors

Dr. Kazim Mirza holds his M.D. from Windsor Medical School, Masters in Teaching from Kaplan University, and Bachelors of Science from Rutgers Honors College. He has taught for 10 years at Kaplan Premier Test Prep and College Admissions, helping countless students achieve their goals and get into their dream schools. Dr. Mirza's expertise is in tutoring for Test Prep, particularly in the areas of prep and ACT prep.

Tana Cabanillas has tutored and FCAT for more than 10 years. She holds a Bachelor of Science degree in Molecular and Microbiology and went on to Windsor University Medical School. Tana was honored in the Top 5% of high school students nationally, and in the National Dean's list in 2004-2005, being among only the top 1% of college students to be honored with this distinction.

Dr. Steve Warner earned his Ph.D. at Rutgers University in Mathematics, and he currently works as an Associate Professor at Hofstra University. Dr. Warner has over 15 years of experience in general math tutoring and over 10 years of experience in math tutoring. He has tutored students both individually and in group settings and has published several math prep books for the SAT, ACT, and AP exams.

OTHER BOOKS FROM GET 800

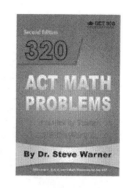

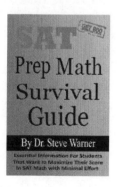
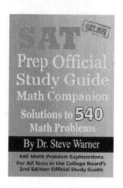
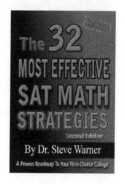

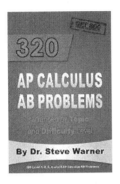
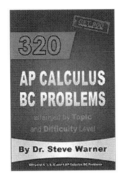

Made in the USA
Lexington, KY
13 April 2016